Praise for **FIRST-GENERATION PROFESSIONALS IN HIGHER EDUCATION**

"This book gives the reader constant opportunities for reflection, tangible examples of experiences seen in various professional environments, and critical steps for first-generation college students as they prepare and navigate becoming or enhancing their professional identities. I certainly wish I had this level of detail during my own 'first-gen' experience."

—**Yolanda Norman,** *Associate Vice President of Student Development, Concordia University Texas*

"*First-generation Professionals in Higher Education* is a comprehensive treatment of the characteristics, needs, and potential of first-generation students and professionals at various stages of educational and professional development. The authors offer a diverse and rich range of perspectives on this important—and often maligned—population. This book should be read and discussed by all types of educators at all types of postsecondary institutions."

—**John N. Gardner,** *Founder and Executive Chair, John N. Gardner Institute for Excellence in Undergraduate Education*

"From the weight of navigating social capital to combating imposter syndrome, our first-generation students become first-generation academics and student affairs professionals. This text uncovers the various ways that this identity manifests throughout their professional experiences in higher education and, more importantly, how we can support and validate them."

—**James K. Winfield,** *Associate Dean for FYE, General Education, and Retention Strategies, Southern New Hampshire University*

"This inspiring book is an authentic and insightful resource for first-generation professionals at all levels. The authors' informative, encouraging, and affirming accounts provide valuable food-for-thought for individuals to reflect on and design their own career paths. A very worthwhile read!"

—**Diana M. Doyle,** *President Emerita,*
Arapahoe Community College

"As a fellow first-generation administrator, I found *First-generation Professionals in Higher Education* extremely validating. The text highlights many important facets related to the first-generation experience and how it translates into our work as student affairs administrators. I would highly recommend this book for graduate students and professionals at all levels."

—**Juan R. Guardia,** *Assistant Vice President for*
Student Affairs and Dean of Students,
University of Cincinnati

"This book validates my personal and professional experiences as a first-generation, Black, female, senior leader. I feel seen, heard, and valued."

—**Kimberly M. Lowry,** *Vice President, Student Success and*
Instruction, Lone Star College–Houston North

FIRST-GENERATION
PROFESSIONALS
IN HIGHER EDUCATION

FIRST-GENERATION PROFESSIONALS IN HIGHER EDUCATION

Strategies for the World of Work

Mary Blanchard Wallace
and Associates

FOREWORD BY **DORIS CHING**

NASPA.
Student Affairs Administrators
in Higher Education

CENTER FOR FIRST-GENERATION STUDENT SUCCESS.
AN INITIATIVE OF NASPA AND THE SUDER FOUNDATION

NASPA.
Student Affairs Administrators
in Higher Education

Published by
NASPA–Student Affairs Administrators in Higher Education
111 K Street, NE
10ᵗʰ Floor
Washington, DC 20002
www.naspa.org

Additional copies may be purchased by contacting the NASPA publications department at 202-265-7500 or visiting http://bookstore.naspa.org.

Library of Congress Cataloging-in-Publication Data
(Prepared by The Donohue Group, Inc.)

Names: Wallace, Mary Blanchard, author. | Ching, Doris (Doris M.), writer of supplementary textual content. | NASPA-Student Affairs Administrators in Higher Education, issuing body.
Title: First-generation professionals in higher education : strategies for the world of work / Mary Blanchard Wallace and associates ; foreword by Doris Ching.
Description: First edition. | Washington, DC : NASPA-Student Affairs Administrators in Higher Education, [2022] | Includes bibliographical references and index.
Identifiers: ISBN 9781948213363 (paperback) | ISBN 9781948213370 (ePub)
Subjects: LCSH: Education, Higher--United States--Employees. | Immigrants--Employment--United States. | Professional employees--United States. | First-generation college students--United States.
Classification: LCC LB2331.68 .W35 2022 (print) | LCC LB2331.68 (ebook) | DDC 378.110973--dc23

Printed and bound in the United States of America

FIRST EDITION

CENTER FOR
FIRST-GENERATION
STUDENT SUCCESS.

AN INITIATIVE OF NASPA AND THE SUDER FOUNDATION

About the Center

The Center for First-generation Student Success, an initiative of NASPA and The Suder Foundation, is the premier source of evidence-based practices, professional development, and knowledge creation for the higher education community to advance the success of first-generation students. Based in Washington, D.C., the Center aims to acknowledge the intersectional experiences of first-generation college students. It offers an outlet for sharing cutting-edge research and current media conversations; opportunities for engagement through online learning, conferences, and events; and access to a bevy of programs and services intended to improve first-generation initiatives across higher education.

A Note of Gratitude

As we continue to grapple with the experiences of first-generation college students, the professional identity of first-generation leaders, scholars, and practitioners emerges for necessary consideration. It is because of *First-generation Professionals in Higher Education: Strategies for the World of Work* that we can further contextualize lived experiences and better support the field. The Center is grateful for the leadership of Mary Blanchard Wallace and the contributions from many influential first-generation leaders for creating a first-of-its-kind, expert resource.

—**SARAH E. WHITLEY**, PhD, Assistant Vice President,
Center for First-generation Student Success, NASPA

CONTENTS

FOREWORD

This book, *First-generation Professionals in Higher Education: Strategies for the World of Work*, has relevance for higher education professionals at all stages of their careers. It is not limited to those who are the first in their family to earn a college degree or the first in their family to be employed in a professional position. The authors' experiences and recommendations presented in these chapters are also broadly applicable to professionals in other fields, both within and outside of higher education.

The book was initiated by Mary Blanchard Wallace, who was inspired by the plethora of support available to entry-level first-generation student affairs faculty and staff. As a first-generation professional herself, Wallace noted throughout her career that colleagues and supervisors noticed her professional assets, such as her work ethic, productivity, and ability to navigate myriad personal and professional relationships. On the other hand, she observed that, when she moved to a mid-level managerial position, she was confronted with situations that required a whole new set of unfamiliar skills. There were times when she experienced real stumbling blocks. Perplexed by her inability to name the reason for her struggles, she discussed her dilemma with her first-generation professional colleagues. She also consulted first-generation college student success counselors and discovered their common patterns of stories and strategies. Motivated by the prospect that her distinct experiences could encourage and benefit others who identify as first-generation professionals, she launched a research agenda on strategies and narratives that might shed an asset-based lens through which to view first-generation professionals' work performance and workstyles. In Wallace's words, "[It is my] hope that other first-generation professionals can use this book to reflect on their pathways, make intentional decisions related to the topics, be inspired to write their own narratives, contribute to the field through research, and aspire to mid-level and senior leadership levels" (M. Wallace, personal communication, July 6, 2020).

There is a striking portrayal distinction between first-generation college students and first-generation higher education professionals. First-generation college students are generally characterized as burdened with academic, social, navigational, financial, and other "deficit" challenges in college. In contrast, first-generation professionals are viewed as successful and striving higher education faculty and staff with personal and professional strengths including empowerment, resilience, financial stability, financial literacy, visionary and strategic leadership skills, political savvy, relationship- and community-building abilities, and other assets. It is through these perspectives that the chapter authors relate their career transitions and their candid practical recommendations.

The authors are acutely experienced. In the interest of intergenerational learning, they readily share their gained knowledge and skills in their career pathways that impacted their personal and professional lives. Through intuition, instincts, and adaptiveness, they learned how to overcome many challenges in order to succeed. This book is evidence that future generations of professionals can learn from and be mentored and enlightened by first-generation professionals who are willing to pass on to others their insights into what helped them attain their goals.

Doris Ching
Emeritus Vice President for Student Affairs
University of Hawai`i System

PART I

Professional Identity

1

First-generation Professionals as Influencers

MARY BLANCHARD WALLACE

irst-generation professionals working in higher education are influencers. Their journeys are varied, but themes of resilience, a strong work ethic, and a connection to community highlight stories of success. The narrative of first-generation students is just beginning to emerge as a story of resilience and persistence framed in strength and asset-based language. Professionals identifying as first-generation college students have always known this, but the story has often been told using deficit language. This book is part of efforts to bring the narrative of first-generation professionals to the forefront of the profession of higher education.

Each author in this book identifies as a first-generation professional: a professional who identified as a first-generation college student and is in the workforce in a position requiring a college education. In particular, this book addresses topics related to first-generation professionals in the field of higher education. The Center for First-generation Student Success (2017), in a blog about defining *first-generation*, stated,

"Ultimately, the term 'first-generation' implies the possibility that a student may lack the critical cultural capital necessary for college success because their parents did not attend college" (para. 5). Components of this definition also apply to first-generation professionals. Having found success as college graduates, first-generation professionals enter careers different than their parents and/or families. First-generation professionals navigating careers in higher education are able to utilize lessons and mentoring from families and from college, enjoying successful careers in higher education. The authors of this book explore some of the complexities of the transition from college/professional school to the work world of higher education, as well as the transition from mid- to senior-level leadership, and how first-generation professionals navigate these transitions.

Framing their chapters in the concepts of capital (Bordieu, 1986; Dumais & Ward, 2010; Yosso, 2005), the contributing authors approach topics of navigating the field of higher education as first-generation professionals through personal experience as well as evidence-based approaches and strategies. For example, as first-generation professionals understand imposter syndrome, mentoring, networking, and politics in the workforce, they become nimble to navigate this new world. Using the lessons learned through college journeys, first-generation professionals are well positioned to succeed in careers requiring college degrees. Yosso's (2005) community cultural wealth model provides an asset-based approach to capital, explored broadly through aspirational, navigational, linguistic, familial, social, and resistant capital. This framework, developed through the tenets of critical race theory, can provide readers background on some of the language the authors use in describing their lived experiences, and provides a way to conceptualize opportunities and challenges for the first-generation professionals working in a higher educational setting. One caution to the reader: The limitation of this approach is that the model was developed as a critical race theory, as a framework for asset language for communities of color (Yosso, 2005). The social cognitive career theory (SCCT; Lent et al., 1994) can also provide a model for the reader to conceptualize the lived experiences of first-generation professionals, from narratives that highlight barriers and deficits to stories of overcoming challenges, centering the experiences of first-generation professionals as stories of strength and excellence.

Authors also explore career progressions of first-generation professionals in higher education. Frameworks will be helpful for readers to reference in relation to career transition and building capital. The SCCT explores the ways in which individuals make decisions about their careers and how these decisions are influenced by personal and environmental variables. Along with the SCCT, the cultural wealth model (Yosso, 2005) also offers a way to think about first-generation professionals' careers, particularly transitions. In Chapter 2 of this book, the author describes the cultural wealth model as a framework for utilizing capital developed throughout one's career. For example, as a first-generation professional transitions to a mid-level career, using one's capital is necessary for success in the field of higher education.

Garriott (2020) posited a critical cultural wealth model of academic and career development for first-generation and economically marginalized students. This model considers elements of capital, similar to Yosso (2005). Garriott's model also explores structural and institutional conditions, social emotional experiences, career self-authorship, and academic/career outcomes. This framework can also apply to first-generation professionals as a way to conceptualize career transition. This model positions institutions as accountable to the limitations of the system for first-generation college students, while representing the individual as impacted by and impacting the institution. The model frames complex interactions between the institution and the individual as a way to understand how the individual navigates the institution. Garriott's model aids the reader of this book to think critically about how first-generation professionals navigate careers in higher education at institutions that are complex and multi-faceted. The model helps the reader to understand transitions for first-generation professionals, particularly navigating mid-level career transitions.

The topics presented in this work are not exhaustive of all transitional issues for first-generation professionals in higher education. Authors approach distinct topics, such as imposter syndrome, networking, mentoring, moving up, and more. These topics are explored through concepts of capital, as defined by Yosso (2005). Readers will explore and discern the strategies most applicable to their situations and desires for transition in the field of higher education.

The book is written with the mid-level first-generation professional in mind. The authors recognize the professional journey sometimes mimics the college journey. First-generation college students sometimes have a plethora of resources, such as mentoring programs, bridge programs, welcome weeks, engaged faculty, and federal TRIO programs, to help them navigate the first year of college. Then, first-generation students are caught in the "sophomore slump" and begin to navigate in completely different ways as they matriculate through the university. Similarly, first-generation professionals use navigational capital built both in their families and in college/graduate school to experience the first several years as a professional in higher education. The mid-level professional transition in higher education presents new challenges, including navigating bureaucracy and politics, managing larger budgets, developing networks to prepare for job transitions, finding sponsors and senior-level mentors, and defining next career steps. This book is a resource for mid-level first-generation professionals, to increase understanding of the topics presented and to encourage them to reflect on their own journey in higher education. As such, each chapter ends with activities, exercises, and/or reflection questions.

Career Progression for a First-generation Professional

The SCCT (Lent et al., 1994) is a framework used to understand how an individual makes career decisions. The SCCT combines two concepts:

1. Career decision frameworks using the lens of social cognitive theory (Bandura, 1986)
2. Interest type theories of career development

The SCCT posits that there is an interlocking and bidirectional relationship between self-efficacy, outcome expectations, and goal representation as individuals make career decisions (Lent et al., 1994). The SCCT allows for the lens of an asset-based approach as we discuss the first-generation professional at the mid-level positions: resilience, growth mindsets, and goal-oriented behaviors. The framework also accounts for personal characteristics, such as race and gender (intersectionality), and environmental variables, such as exposure to careers and decisions. This framework is helpful to understand the journey of the mid-level first-generation higher education professional, as well as their career advancement. Concepts of the SCCT are included throughout this book, as the authors explore issues such as imposter syndrome (self-efficacy), resilience (outcome expectations and goal representations), and intersectional identities (personal characteristics).

Research focused on career transition for first-generation higher education professionals is emerging. One sector we can examine is government. A recent study completed for the Department of Commerce by the U.S. Census Bureau (Terry & Fobia, 2019) employed a qualitative research design, utilizing the SCCT to identify barriers and assets that first-generation professionals experience during career transitions in the "white collar" world of work. Though this study is not generalizable to the population of first-generation professionals (qualitative research methods and data are not, typically), there are some lessons we can glean from the results. Researchers found that first-generation professionals in government experience barriers to networking, finding mentors, developing professional pathways to gain experience, and navigating authority structures. Researchers also found great strength demonstrated by first-generation professionals: grit (resilience), a strong work ethic, and the ability to prove themselves. Study participants articulated support structures that are helpful for success in governmental positions: extended orientations, assignment of a mentor, and leadership training at the mid-level. More research is needed to understand supportive structures for first-generation professionals in higher education.

Olson (2014) identified challenges and assets of first-generation college graduates, and used Lent et al.'s (1994, 2000) SCCT framework to understand these students' career transitions immediately after graduation. Presenting the SCCT framework, Olson studied a first-generation college student's early career, exploring concepts of self-efficacy, outcome expectations, and goals, while reminding the reader of the supports and barriers for students as they navigate college. Olson described resources that assist first-generation graduates, including visiting with a career counselor. A career counselor can help students identify self-efficacy perceptions. Olson's model aids the reader of this book in recognizing resources needed to navigate mid-level career transitions as a first-generation professional in higher education. Resources include mentoring, relationship building, understanding institutions, and skills development.

Social Capital and Applications for First-generation Community

This book explores and identifies strategies for first-generation professionals to use capital in maneuvering workplaces, particularly higher education. The two components of the community cultural wealth model applied to first-generation professionals in this book include aspirational and navigational capital. Yosso (2005) defined these concepts in the following ways:

- *Aspirational capital* – "Refers to the ability to maintain hopes and dreams for the future, even in the face of real and perceived barriers" (p. 77)
- *Navigational capital* – "Refers to skills of maneuvering through social institutions" (p. 80)

Yosso identified other forms of capital in the community cultural wealth model, which the reader will encounter in this book as authors explore how they developed capital through lived experiences and how developing this capital was impacted by being a first-generation professional. These other forms of capital defined by Yosso (2005) include the following:

- *Linguistic capital* – "intellectual and social skills attained through communication experiences in more than one language and/or style" (p. 78)
- *Familial capital* – "cultural knowledges nurtured among *familia* [kin] that carry a sense of community history, memory and cultural intuition" (p. 79)
- *Social capital* – "networks of people and community resources" (p. 79)
- *Resistant capital* – "knowledges and skills fostered through oppositional behavior that challenges inequality" (p. 80)

The authors also describe intersections of their identities (e.g., gender, race, socioeconomic status, sexual identity, urban, rural), expanding the reader's understanding of their lived experience of being a first-generation professional in higher education. First-generation professionals are all different, and they do not necessarily experience institutions or career transitions in the same way. Intersectionality of identity impacts social capital, as described in Yosso's (2005) work.

How to Use This Book

This book is organized in three sections:

- Section I: Professional Identity
- Section II: Purposeful Interaction
- Section III: Career Paths

Navigating describes a variety of strategies the authors utilize to advance and experience the student affairs profession. This book applies Yosso's (2005) concept of navigational capital to the mid-level higher education professional. Institutions of higher education are complex organizations and social institutions. Yosso (2005) addressed navigating institutions, identifying the asset of resilience that individuals develop through difficult situations.

Each chapter ends with questions and/or activities. These questions and activities serve as a starting point for the reader to reflect on the topics addressed in the chapter. The authors of this book intend to assist the reader in using reflection to develop their own leadership capacity and capital. Lent et al. (1994) posited that thinking about and "constructing meaning" is a critical piece of career development, stating, "Constructivist theories emphasize cognitive feed-forward (as opposed to feedback-only) mechanisms, highlighting the importance of anticipation, forethought and active construction of meaning in interaction with environmental events" (p. 87). For this reason, the reader should consider treating the reflection and activities sections of each chapter as opportunities to make meaning of their own career journey as a first-generation professional in higher education.

Section I focuses on developing professional identity. Authors present their own narratives of strength, and present topics related to transitioning in mid-level careers. This section invites the reader to think critically about their personal strengths and abilities. Chapter 1 introduces the book, inviting the reader to think about first-generation identity and career development. In Chapter 2, the author describes imposter syndrome and how it shows up for a first-generation professional in higher education. Using Yosso's cultural wealth model (2005), the author takes the reader on a journey to discover true strength as a first-generation professional. Chapter 3 reminds the reader that first-generation professionals in higher education navigate institutions that can be bureaucratic and political, as defined by Bolman and Deal (2017). The author offers a technique to build relationships as one transitions through mid-level career paths. Finally, Chapter 4 presents practical financial literacy and lessons needed to navigate personal financial situations, and identifies the milestones for financial stability as one progresses through a career in higher education. Readers should consider the following questions as they read Section I:

- What common family expectations do first-generation professionals experience?
- How do these familial expectations differ among first-generation professionals?
- How do these expectations impact the professional identities of first-generation professionals?
- How do first-generation professionals experience imposter syndrome?
- How do first-generation professionals learn about the political framework of higher education, and further, how do they navigate bureaucratic organizations, like colleges and universities?
- How do first-generation professionals learn about money management, both personally and professionally? Further,

how does this impact their work with large and complex budget structures in professional roles?

Section II tackles topics related to navigating the interactions of a mid-level professional in higher education. This section invites the reader to ponder strategies to utilize as they consider the network of supportive professionals in higher education, especially in the transition from mid-level to upper-management or executive-level leadership roles. Topics such as the resilience of first-generation professionals, building community with "capable others" that facilitate professional growth (in academic and administrative departments), and the importance of mentoring for first-generation professionals are addressed. Section II begins with Chapter 5, in which the authors examine resilience and intersectionality. The chapter explores resiliency as a strength of first-generation professionals, and how resilience leads to success as one transitions to the mid-level positions in higher education. Chapter 6 discusses how to build professional networks for mid-level professionals and ultimately how to leverage these networks for career success. Understanding how to build and sustain these networks is imperative for all professionals in higher education, but even more so for the first-generation professional. Chapter 7 focuses on mentoring and being a mentor, especially as one reaches mid-level career success. How does one both find a mentor and become a mentor for others? Readers should consider the following questions as they read this section:

- What is your story of resilience? How is resilience taxing for a first-generation professional, especially at all intersections of identity?
- How do first-generation professionals navigate networking? Is it different from the way continuing-generation professionals navigate these communities? To which communities do

first-generation professional have access? Which communities are difficult for first-generation professionals to access?

- How does a mentoring relationship develop? Is it important for first-generation professionals to identify mentors? Is it important for first-generation professionals to serve as mentors?

Section III explores career pathways and career development, tackling issues from the job search to executive-level career success. Chapter 8 frames the job search for a career in higher education, particularly as first-generation professionals move through entry, mid-level, and senior leadership. The authors use the specialized language of these pathways, and describe the skill sets, competencies, and political capital first-generation professionals need to navigate their careers. In Chapter 9, readers are introduced to first-generation faculty who champion the first-generation experience as what led to career success in academia. Chapter 10 describes pathways to becoming a college or university president, and includes lessons learned and resources to reach career success. Readers should consider the following questions as they read this section:

- How do first-generation professionals prepare for a job search? What skills must they develop prior to engaging in a job search in higher education?
- How does a first-generation professional craft a narrative about their experiences to use in job interviews and professional communities?
- How do first-generation professionals use their capital to leverage careers in senior-level administration?
- How are faculty uniquely positioned to be champions for the first-generation community?

Rural Roots and a Cajun Family Expectation: Mary's Narrative

In each chapter, authors share insights into their own journeys as a way to claim their narratives as ones of strength and asset to the field of higher education. My own narrative starts with growing up in a small Cajun town in southern Louisiana. My parents grew up with the effects of the Great Depression, and thus imparted many lessons about the value of the dollar and of higher education. I was very aware of my parents' hopes and dreams for my future. Their expectations were high, and in turn, so were mine.

My father and mother owned a small, independent hardware store. It was in my family's hardware store that I learned the value of work, as my siblings and I cleaned and stocked shelves, counted inventory, and ran the cash register. We were all expected to pitch in at the store and at home. Idleness was not tolerated, and typically punished. This expectation of a high work ethic came from all levels of my family: great grandparents, grandparents, parents, and others. My entire town thrived on working hard and coming together as a community. The mantra "Early to bed, early to rise makes a man healthy, wealthy, and wise" became the record of my childhood. When I got my first job in high school as a receptionist at a doctor's office, my mother told me, "If there is nothing else to do, empty the trash." This served as a lesson to always be working, and that no job was beneath me. My mother also taught me to leave things better than I found them. In addition, the consistent message I received from my parents, particularly my father, was, "I work hard labor in my job so one day you can go to college and not need to do this."

My father's hopes and dreams for my future propelled me to do my best in school. I had a sense of aspiration that was embedded in my family's expectation that I attend college. I believed I had two choices for a career: nurse or teacher. In my small town, these are what most of the professional women became, and they seemed to be my only possibilities. Because I helped care for my grandmother, who lived with my family, I felt called to become a nurse. It made sense that I would earn a Bachelor of Science in nursing, become a registered nurse, and return to my hometown to practice as a nurse and live near my family. Not only did I believe this is what I would do; it was expected. I knew my family was counting on me to become the first in the family to attend college, and one of the few of my Brusly High School graduating class to leave home to pursue higher learning.

I never became a nurse or K–12 teacher. When I came back home from graduate school where I studied college student personnel, even though my parents never really understood my job titles, they always made it clear how proud they were of me. I also had much confusion and misunderstanding about my career pathway. For example, when I showed my mother the new pair of blue jeans I bought to wear to my first professional conference, she said, "You cannot wear jeans, Mary. This is not a hardware conference." I was embarrassed that I did not understand the mores of my new profession. Within hours, my seamstress mother sewed a simple pair of slacks and paired it with a silk blouse out of her closet. Looking back on that moment, I now understand that I was still developing and understanding the hidden curriculum of my new work: the dress code. I also think of that moment as yet another time my mother sacrificed her aspirations for my own. I knew my mother aspired to several careers that would require a college degree. She once told me she wanted to be a teacher or a 4-H extension agent. When I asked her why she never attended college, she would shrug her shoulders and say, "I'm making sure you get your college degree. That's enough for me." This was a common theme with my parents throughout my life—sacrifice for their children's education.

As I embarked on my career, my father reminded me who I was and where I came from. After my doctoral graduation, the first thing my father said to me was, "Dr. Wallace, don't forget your roots." This reminder of who I was in my family helped me to stay humble, even as I climbed the career ladder in higher education. At the same time, my father would tell all of his friends, "Mary is the president of all the students at that university!" I was only an associate director of housing at the time, but I never corrected him because I did not know how to explain my work to him. The intersection of pride for my accomplishments and the desire for me to remember my upbringing from my father always drove me to stay grounded and move forward at the same time.

Conclusion

Family expectations and encouragement, balanced with a healthy dose of navigational capital, is a familiar story for many first-generation professionals. The authors' narratives in this book are intertwined with seasoned advice and reflection for mid-level first-generation professionals as they navigate their own journey through higher education.

Questions for Reflection

Each chapter in this book provides the reader with an opportunity to dig deeper into the complexity and strength of being a first-generation professional. The following questions will help readers set the stage for the reflections and exercises throughout the book:

- What is your first-generation professional identity? Where do your identities intersect, and how does this impact your professional journey?
- What strengths do you bring to your profession? Describe a situation when being a first-generation professional brought strength and capital to your work.
- What do you hope to gain from reading this book? How do you think this book will assist you in your career journey?
- What do you hope to give as a first-generation professional? What is your plan to do so?
- What are your career aspirations, and how do you plan to reach them? How do you believe your first-generation identity can help you achieve these aspirations?

References

Bandura, A. (1986). *Social foundations of thought and action: A social cognitive theory.* Prentice Hall.

Bolman, L. G., & Deal, T. E. (2017). *Reframing organizations: Artistry, choice, and leadership* (6th ed). Wiley & Sons.

Bordieu, P. (1986). The forms of capital. In J. Richardson (Ed.), *Handbook of theory and research for the sociology of education* (pp. 241–258). Greenwood Press.

Center for First-generation Student Success. (2017, November 20). Defining first-generation. *The Center for First-generation Student Success Blog.* https://firstgen.naspa.org/blog/defining-first-generation

Dumais, S. A., & Ward, A. (2010). Cultural capital and first-generation college success. *Poetics, 38*(3), 245–265. https://doi.org/10.1016/j.poetic.2009.11.011

Garriott, P. O. (2020). A critical cultural wealth model of first-generation and economically marginalized college students' academic and career development. *Journal of Career Development, 47*(1), 80–95. https://doi.org/10.1177/0894845319826266

Lent, R. W., Brown, S. D., & Hackett, G. (1994). Toward a unifying social cognitive theory of career and academic interest, choice, and performance [Monograph]. *Journal of Vocational Behavior, 45*(1), 79–122. https://doi.org/10.1006/jvbe.1994.1027

Lent, R. W., Brown, S. D., & Hackett, G. (2000). Contextual supports and barriers to career choice: A social cognitive analysis. *Journal of Counseling Psychology, 47*(1), 36–49. https://doi.org/10.1037/0022-0167.47.1.36

Olson, J. S. (2014). Opportunities, obstacles, and options: First-generation college graduates and social cognitive career theory. *Journal of Career Development, 41*(3), 199–217. https://doi.org/10.1177/0894845313486352

Terry, R. L., & Fobia, A. C. (2019). *Qualitative research on barriers to workplace inclusion for first generation professionals* (Research Report Series, Survey Methodology #2019-03). U.S. Census Bureau. http://www.census.gov/content/dam/Census/library/working-papers/2019/adrm/rsm2019-03.pdf

Yosso, T. J. (2005). Whose culture has capital? A critical race theory discussion of community cultural wealth. *Race Ethnicity and Education, 8*(1), 69–91. https://doi.org/10.1080/1361332052000341006

2

Imposter Syndrome Revisited

A Journey of Learning and Unlearning

D'ANDRA MULL

This chapter offers an overview of the manifestation, the effect, and the impact of imposter syndrome on many first-generation students and professionals. I weave my own narrative throughout, discussing both foundational intersections and compounding factors of my journey and experience with imposter syndrome. The chapter also contextualizes imposter syndrome as it relates to an individual's sense of agency and mobility; I discuss the impacts of social and cultural capital, arguing that they should be seen not as a deficit but as a dividend of community cultural wealth (Yosso, 2005). I also address the significance and implications of changing the narrative for future generations and introduce tangible approaches to navigating the profession. The chapter concludes with an opportunity for self-reflection through guided questions, and I offer strategies for overcoming feelings of imposter syndrome.

As a first-generation college graduate preparing to author this contribution, I reviewed the existing literature and immediately saw myself and my journey—as an undergraduate, graduate, and doctoral student, and particularly as a new and emerging professional—reflected in the experiences shared there. Today, as a sitting vice president at one of the top public schools in the United States, I recognize not only how imposter syndrome manifested itself in my life but also how I have worked to unlearn that false narrative I once constructed for myself. I now better understand the many ways in which I navigated and pivoted due to experience I possessed, not lacked. I honor the important stories and scholarship that enabled many first-generation professionals to give voice to anxieties they have struggled to name while navigating brave new worlds of higher education and professions beyond the academy. We successfully endeavor forward—not as imposters, but as skilled contributors in spaces not always constructed with our lenses and experiences in mind.

Imposter Syndrome

"Uh oh, they're going to find out now. I've run a game on everybody and they're going to find me out." —Maya Angelou

For more than 4 decades, researchers and scholars have worked to give voice to the phenomenon of imposter syndrome (Bernard et al., 2002; Clance & Imes, 1978; Ewing et al., 1996; Hutchins, 2015; Kumar & Jagacinski, 2006; Naumann et al., 2003). *Imposter syndrome,* also called *imposter phenomenon* and *imposterism,* refers to the unfounded internal belief or feeling among high-achieving individuals that their accomplishments are beyond their control and are instead the result of luck, external factors, intellectual deception, or fraudulence (Clance & O'Toole, 1988; Gibson-Beverly & Schwartz, 2008). Those with imposter syndrome assign their success to the grace and kindness of others; some even attribute it to others' lack of judgement or false belief in their abilities or skills (Chakraverty, 2019). Imposter syndrome, in turn, limits one's ability to internalize success—in fact, it leads a person to fear or undermine their accomplishments (Bernard et al., 2002; Cokley et al., 2013).

Figure 2.1

Diagram Illustrating the Imposter Cycle (Based on Clance, 1985)

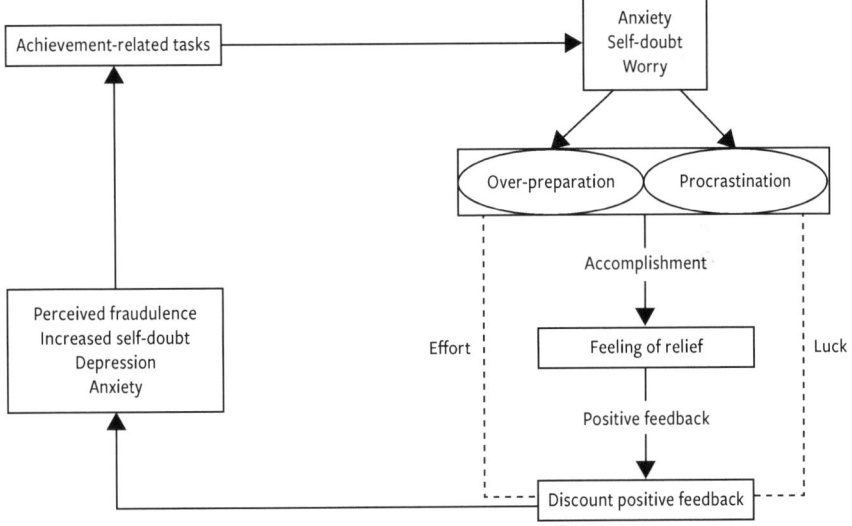

Note. The cycle begins with the assignment of achievement related tasks.

As illustrated in Figure 2.1 and outlined in Clance's (1985) early research on imposter syndrome, the phenomenon often occurs when assignments or tasks are doled out and leads to a continuous cycle of self-doubt coupled with either overpreparation or procrastination. For many people, this cycle does not impede their ability to complete their work; however, it does cause a good deal of added stress and anxiety, which results in strong feelings of fraudulence, self-doubt, depression, and anxiety (Clance & Imes, 1978). For some experiencing imposter syndrome, overpreparation or procrastination reaffirms beliefs that luck or extremely hard work as the reason they could complete a task (Thompson et al., 2000). Ultimately, when a task is accomplished, there may be some solace, yet it is often temporary—despite evidence of satisfactory work or positive feedback, the struggle to internalize success simply continues.

Although Clance and Imes (1978) theorized imposter syndrome was primarily experienced by women, more recent studies have found that women and men encounter this phenomenon at comparable rates (Bernard et al., 2002; McClain et al., 2016). Women, however, are likely to experience imposter syndrome more intensely than men (Settles et al., 2013). Imposterism has been studied in multiple populations and settings and has been noted to affect numerous individuals and groups (Clance, 1985), including undergraduate and graduate students (Bussotti, 1990); academics (Topping, 1983); medical professionals (Mattie et al., 2008); and women in STEM fields (Trefts, 2019). Researchers estimate that 70% of people will experience imposter syndrome at some point in their lifetime (Gravois, 2007). As such, new studies continue to emerge and inform our understanding of this phenomenon.

Imposter Syndrome in First-generation Populations

First-generation college students are a group distinctly affected by imposter syndrome (Ishitani, 2006; Terenzini et al., 1996), and there are still many dynamics to be studied in relation to the cohort. Defined as individuals whose parents do not have a college degree (Dika & D'Amico, 2016), first-generation students often encounter complexities not faced by their non-first-generation peers (Terenzini et al., 1996). Research has found that imposter syndrome is often heightened and undergirded by social, environmental, and historical challenges that these students must navigate (Cokley et al., 2013). Because 25% of undergraduate college students in the United States are first-generation college students (Dika & D'Amico, 2016), research, scholarship, and vignettes focused on framing imposter syndrome are integral in both centering and strengthening our collective understanding of the experiences this group must navigate as pioneers. It is critical that they—and we as a professional and scholarly community—continue to work to understand how imposter syndrome reveals itself in relation to economic, cultural, and social capital (Gardner & Holley, 2011) and community cultural wealth (Yosso, 2005). Only then can we best empower, champion, and support first-generation professionals as well as remove barriers and impediments to their success.

Imposterism's constant cycle of believing that there is something yet to be proven or unmasked contributes to self-notions of intellectual phoniness—and is seen at significantly higher levels in first-generation college students when compared with other groups (Martinez et al., 2009; Terenzini et al., 1996). Research has shown that these students and graduates, beyond navigating feelings of uncertainty and self-doubt, may not have the same systems of support, resources, or understanding as non-first-generation students. Because they are the first in their family to pursue higher education (Bui, 2002), they also have less knowledge of what to expect in college, and they possess less economic, social, and cultural capital (Bourdieu, 1986). When compared with non-first-generation graduates, first-generation students of color had notably higher imposter phenomenon scores, which significantly correlated with increased depression and anxiety (Peteet et al., 2015). This effect is compounded in students and professionals that are also ethnic minorities. In addition to experiencing racial, ethnic, and gender discrimination, students in this group are more likely to be the first in their family to attend college and often come from families of lower socioeconomic status than other student groups (Bui, 2002).

Manifestation of Imposter Syndrome

"I don't just study imposterism; I experienced it. I inhabited it. It was like a little house I lived in. Of course, no one else knew I was there. It was my secret. . . . If you don't tell anyone about those feelings, then people are less likely to think, 'Hmm . . . maybe she doesn't really deserve to be here.' No need to give them any ideas, right?" —Amy Cuddy, *Presence*

Feelings of imposterism may resonate with you personally. Perhaps you have worked tirelessly to achieve your goals, overcome obstacles, and build the skills and competencies that serve you well in your career. You also hold the distinction of being the first in your family to earn a college degree, and you are now the standard bearer for generations to come. You are the trailblazer and role model—and your path is now charted toward the pursuit and realization of new career opportunities. It is your time.

So off you go. Professionally, you are moving along quite well. This is what you labored to build and achieve. You smile, do good work, and accept new challenges and opportunities. Yet deep down, you may have a nagging concern: You are worried that one day, you are going to be exposed as not belonging or deserving of your seat at the table. You fear that your success may be due to a lucky break and, someday, somebody is going to unmask you. You question yourself: Am I qualified for the job I have, or am I pretending? Should I even be in this room? New opportunities bring doubt, and you worry that your accomplishment is a fluke (Clance & Imes, 1978).

You are by no means a fraud, yet imposter syndrome is experienced by many in our profession. For first-generation students, it may show up when we ponder our sense of belonging and agency as we navigate new spaces and frameworks (Craddock et al., 2011). I have experienced it many times. I have questioned myself and how I got here. Like you, I worked hard, broke cycles, and secured my seat at the table, but I fully acknowledge the many occasions when I felt like I did not belong. I credited others for "giving" me opportunities, even when those individuals pushed back and reminded me that I earned those rewards; they were not given to me. I shorted myself credit—a lot. After a great amount of self-reflection, learning, and unlearning, I have now come to champion myself and appreciate how I got here. But it took time and acknowledging the origins of my self-doubts.

> *"Any moment, someone's going to find out I'm a total fraud, and that I don't deserve any of what I've achieved."* —Emma Watson, *Rookie Magazine*

I can vividly remember the day I earned my doctorate degree. I ambitiously moved through my program in less than 3 years, and my family and friends showed up in droves to attend the ceremony at the university's football stadium. On that day, I officially became the first member of my family to have earned not only a bachelor's degree, but a doctorate. It was a shared accomplishment in the largest of ways. I smiled brightly as I was hooded by my advisor and then proudly strutted across the stage and shook the hand of our university president, the commencement speaker, and, finally, my mentor—the vice president for student affairs with whom I would begin my full-time career two short days later, in a position he created specifically for me. It was the most accomplished I ever felt in my life. Nothing could have possibly wiped the smile from my face.

Yet, just 24 short hours later, I sat in my room and cried for no less than an hour straight as I wondered what I had just done. I graduated with a great sense of pride, yet it was initially short-lived due to my own feelings of inadequacy. I pondered what was yet to come. I was scared to begin my new role, so I began to truly overprepare for what should have been a relaxed and exploratory period of transition (Solórzano et al., 2000). Wiping my tears away, I read everything I could find to prepare for my new professional space. I printed off copies of organizational charts. I reread my job description. I reviewed websites and policies. I had to be beyond ready.

But then it really hit me: I still had questions that could not be answered by a website or found in a job description. How was I really supposed to show up as a worthy professional? I was fearfully certain that somebody—actually, everybody—would know that I was not supposed to be there with them. I had always been able to draw from my experiences to find a path forward, but in that moment, I realized I had no idea how you were supposed to "act" once you earned your doctorate degree or started a new profession.

I came to understand my experience better as I learned how, in academic settings, imposter syndrome can be swiftly triggered when someone transitions from the role of student to that of a faculty or staff member (Knights & Clarke, 2014); this is the case even for students with a strong sense of self and agency (Crenshaw, 1991). The phenomenon has also been noted to appear often after a significant accomplishment, such as being admitted to a prestigious university, winning an award, or earning a promotion. I had experienced the same feelings of doubt when I began my graduate studies as a first-generation college student. Now, I was a young adult with a PhD, expected to navigate the world as a new professional, and I recognized how uneasy I felt in moving forward. I felt as though I could not confide in even my closest friends because I was supposed to have life figured out: After all, I, like so many of my peers, had succeeded in spite of obstacles in my path (Cisco, 2020; Cope-Watson & Betts, 2010). My self-imposed expectations made me believe that I now possessed all the tools and educational credentials to make my way forward. Right? Being a young, highly educated Black woman meant that I was ready for the world, right? Right?

I felt I was not. Back then, though I could not clearly articulate why, I was terrified my colleagues would immediately see someone only pretending to know the unfamiliar path forward. I would later come to understand that the capital many of my more privileged peers used to navigate the world did not exist in the same social, cultural, or economic frames for me (Bourdieu, 1986). I did not have generational footholds of educational attainment firmly guiding my path, yet I knew the expectations were high. Although my family, friends, and community proudly and loudly cheered me every step of the way, they did not have the lived experiences to help advise me on the journey that lay ahead (Hurtado, 1994; Terenzini et al., 1996; Walpole, 2003). I did not come from money. In fact, my entire education had been funded by academic scholarships, pivotal assistantships, and grants. Mentors who looked like me and had walked the same path were few and far between. I was the first—and as such, a fish out of water, scared that my luck had finally run out.

I would experience such cycles of thinking several times throughout my life. In my mind, I operated as a stranger in a foreign land and anxiously dreaded when and how I would be unmasked (Clance, 1985; Craddock et al., 2011; Harvey & Katz, 1985). Imposter syndrome had effectively made its presence known. Today, I now understand how deeply it manifested itself in my thoughts and my actions as I made sense of what it meant to be a new professional navigating new terrains—but I also have a far deeper understanding of how I developed and applied intersecting forms of capital available to me throughout my experiences to help drive my success.

Economic, Cultural, and Social Capital

"Stop focusing on what you are not." —Unknown

Imposter syndrome in first-generation professionals can be brought on by the presence or absence of several factors, including structural barriers. Access, or lack thereof, to different forms of capital is one such lens through which to view various experiences. By leaning into the conceptual framework of Bourdieuian capital, which posits that how individuals generate economic, social, and cultural capital is heavily shaped by financial means, academic qualifications, and communities (Bourdieu, 1986), we get a clearer understanding of the ways many students navigate the academy. But for others, including many first-generation professionals, the framework provides context for the ways in which their paths diverge. Although capital generally represents constructs of influence, economic capital specifically denotes material assets that are "immediately and directly convertible into money and may be institutionalized in the form of property rights" (Bourdieu, 1986, p. 242) and that allow generational upward mobility. Home and property ownership, family trusts, stocks, and other financial assets afford access to power and open doors; such financial security was inherited, created through education attainment, or built via strong investments and financial interactions. Economic capital provides for the funding of and access to education, books, home computers, family vacations, cars, and other provisions, and it creates pathways for success.

Bourdieu (1986) defined *social capital* as the "aggregate of the actual or potential resources that are linked to possession of a durable network of more or less institutionalized relationships of mutual acquaintance and recognition—in other words, to membership in a group" (p. 103). For instance, social organizations—such as country clubs, sorority and fraternity networks, youth leagues, college parent associations, and travel clubs—afford structure and access that increase engagement opportunities for individuals and families. Discussions regarding, for example, where someone's child plans to attend college, career decisions, and a host of other topics emerge to increase resources and expand the network of influence and interactions for group members, which ultimately boosts their social capital. For many first-generation professionals, such social capital may be limited, as interactions with members to these groups may not exist in volumes equal to those who have established family legacies in higher education.

Inroads made through social capital then create ways for additional assets, such as cultural capital, to form. Cultural capital is the accumulation of insider knowledge, norms, skills, expectations, and abilities that allow someone to successfully navigate a larger set of situations, networks, and communities; it, too, increases social mobility (Bourdieu, 1986; Perna, 2006; Walpole, 2003). By enabling a person to understand how to dress, talk, act, and maneuver, cultural capital can boost social mobility, advantage, and sense of belonging. Access to exclusive resources such as tutors, test preparation courses, advanced placement classes, and home computers—all of which can offer informal preparation for understanding and navigating academic culture—enable gatekeeping on the pathway to college and beyond.

Community Cultural Wealth

"It's time for you to make the contribution you were born to make." —Marie Forleo, *http://www.marieforleo.com*

Scholars have interpreted Bourdieu's work in several ways, including as a deficit theory that highlights communities as either wealthy or poor in a hierarchical society that reinforces the status quo (Bourdieu & Passeron, 1979). The limitation of such an analysis in the context of first-generation college students and graduates is that it often disregards the agency, aptitude, and resourcefulness of these individuals and instead positions them as distressed and deficient rather than capable and competent seekers of knowledge and capital—even when they face imposter syndrome. To better understand the experiences of this group, a redefining of cultural capital itself is necessary. It is critical that we recognize and acknowledge that first-generation students and graduates often draw upon a frame of resources different from those given in the Bourdieu model, as posited by Yosso's (2005) theory of community cultural wealth.

Yosso's (2005) community cultural wealth model, as illustrated in Figure 2.2, punctuates Bourdieu's scholarship and provides a different framework for how many people navigate and mitigate imposter syndrome in the academy and beyond. She posited culture as "behaviors and values that are learned, shared, and exhibited by a group of people" (Yosso, 2005, p. 75) and not simply as capital that is passed down or inherited. Contextualized initially to shed light on the educational experiences of communities of color, Yosso's theoretical framework serves to shift the narrative of the deficit model to instead focus on the characteristics that strengthen—rather than stigmatize—underserved groups and persons. I wholly acknowledge how centered I felt in my own experiences after reading Yosso's scholarship: For the first time, I felt that someone understood my story. Moreover, for the first time, I could truly articulate how I navigate the professional settings I have inhabited—in spite of my feelings of imposterism. Finally, I could tell others how I had found my way when I was a novice in so many respects.

Figure 2.2

Diagram Illustrating the Community Cultural Wealth Model (Yosso, 2005)

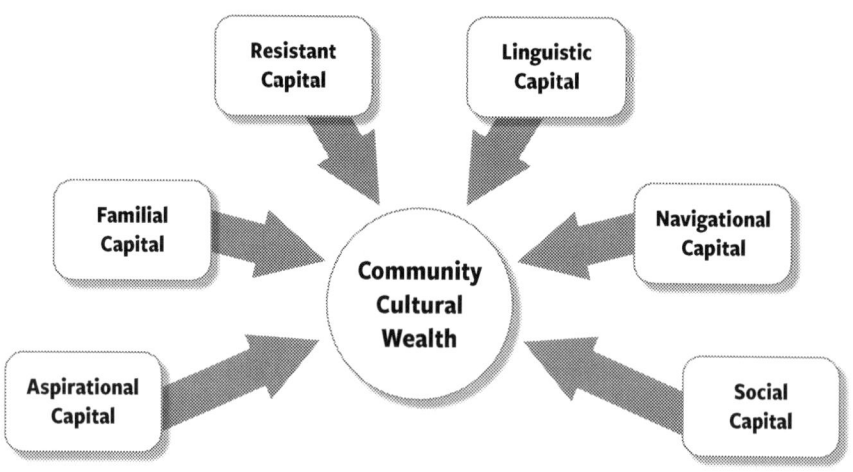

The community cultural wealth model (Yosso, 2005) features aspects of thriving as an individual and community, despite micro- and macro-oppressions present in personal interactions and in the systems individuals navigate. The six-pronged theory of aspirational, navigational, linguistic, familial, social, and resistant capital sees cultural wealth as moving beyond wealth- and status-based traits consistently connected to White, middle-class American values; instead, it acknowledges the assets that are often ignored or undervalued for marginalized groups. Yosso's model postulates that underserved communities engage their inherent strengths and ways of knowing— which do not focus on entitlements as capital, but rather environments and experiences—to navigate educational institutions and beyond, even in the face of self-doubt and fear.

Aspirational Capital

Dream big and aim high. Over the course of my life, I have uttered that phrase to myself more times than I can begin to count. My third-grade teacher challenged me to do both, and I have carried her words of empowerment in my head and in my spirit ever since. I wrote the phrase on my notebook on the first day of classes during each year of high school. My family always told me that if I worked hard, I could achieve anything. I believed them. My neighbor would call me over regularly to ask how school was going, and she would give me a few dollars for "keeping my head on straight and doing the right thing." We did not have a lot of money in my family or community, but that did not matter. I knew that college was the next step for me, and I prepared with that end in mind. I had a village of support championing me along the way. I took accelerated classes. I participated in the academic college bowl. I was a high school athlete. I was president of the student body. Yet, even then, I often felt like an outsider in my predominately White high school. I remember when, during my freshman year, the four names of our school's representatives for the academic college bowl were announced. I beamed when my name was called. Later, an upperclassman passed me in the hallway and commented that he did not know I was "that smart." I remember wondering to myself whether my election was indeed a fluke or a lucky break. That was the first time I can recall feeling like an imposter, yet I also heard the voice of my grandmother in my head as she told me she was proud of me, and I reflected on the words of my teacher: *Dream big and aim high*. That was the moment I knew, indeed, that I was "that smart" and that the messages I received throughout my life figured greatly into my ability and desire to *dream big and aim high*. Our team would go on to place third in the state competition my first year, and, by my senior year, we would take home the first-place prize.

For first-generation professionals like me, *aspirational capital* is often seen in a family's, community's, or individual's determination to achieve—even when resources are limited or the path forward is unclear—and such capital remains a critical reinforcer of what students can achieve as they progress. When barriers, whether real or perceived, emerge, resiliency takes over; hopes and goals remain in place for not only students but also their parents (Yosso, 2005). As the scholarship of Gándara (1995) attested, aspirational capital opens up new possibilities—first-generation professionals recognize that educational attainment creates opportunities, resources, and career paths unavailable to other members of their family. A new means to create a legacy of excellence is seen; hope is transferred from one generation to another, used to support students throughout their journey and even when they are faced with structural inequality and the perception of being an outsider (Yosso, 2005). Imposter syndrome still may rear its head, but a strong sense of aspirational capital also emerges as a counter-message. Such messages of inspiration are foundational and a family's pride in their student is magnified despite structural and institutional barriers—including financial barriers, racism, unequal access to resources, and bias—that exist. Ultimately, the individual recognizes what is important and at stake for them and for their extended family and community.

Navigational Capital

As my high school career was winding down, I thought about what my life would hold as I set off to begin a new chapter. I went through high school with only five other Black women in my honors and advanced placement cohort. We were figuring things out together. Five of the six of us had no idea what "college" looked like, but we were determined to find out. We had fears, but we also had each other. We endeavored to create new pathways and models of success for our families and ourselves. We worried about how we would fit into the next stage of our lives, but we constantly shared information regarding application deadlines, fee waivers, new scholarship offerings, and college visitation days. We would take the earlier bus to school so that we could arrive an hour before our peers and talk about things we discovered during the college search process. We visited universities, and we talked about what we wanted as we dreamed of what was coming next. Some of us would attend large, public, land-grant institutions; another would be drawn to the legacy of excellence afforded by historically Black colleges and universities; and one would take full advantage of a 4-year academic scholarship she received in the sixth grade and put it to great use. All six of us received substantial financial aid awards that removed the heavy burden of trying to figure out how we would pay for it all. All of us were a bit afraid and unsure, but mostly we were excited because we knew that all we worked for would soon be within reach. Today, of the six of us, three have earned doctoral degrees, two have earned law degrees, and one is a fire chief in a large city. We held each other accountable and knew, even as teenagers, that no woman would be left behind. We curiously peered down the road ahead, together. We did not know or fully comprehend the path, but we knew it was forward. And yes—I would feel like an imposter on the first day I set foot in a college classroom, but I aspired to achieve despite my uncertainty. I, like my friends, desired more. I had no clue until years later, but I would learn that it was my engagement of aspirational capital that allowed me to push through my feelings of fraudulence in this new world.

I often reached out to my high school girlfriends as I navigated my insecurities and found my way forward. We talked about the sororities we were thinking about joining. Five of us would do so, and our newfound sisterhood would provide us with a robust world of resources and knowledge. We would share information regarding summer internship programs and job opportunities, as we all needed the money. We would talk about what we learned over the course of each semester and share academic resources. We related what not to do when filling out federal financial aid forms, and we passed along information about new scholarship opportunities. As our under-graduate careers wrapped up, we also talked about what made us uneasy about entering our graduate or career fields. We were nervous and unsure of what the next stage of life would look like, yet we were finding our way forward and steering new courses.

Navigational capital can counteract imposter syndrome when individuals leverage the skills they developed by maneuvering in social institutions, including higher education environments created without underserved communities in mind (Yosso, 2005). For first-generation professionals, navigational capital is engaged when they activate their own sense of agency to complete college applications and financial aid forms; register for standardized tests; schedule courses; and undertake a host of other unfamiliar, yet critical, edu-cational activities. Unlike dominant cultures, this group must use its own skills to access the same institutions and opportunities without the help of others who have gone before and can show them the way. When faced with stressful events, environments, and circumstances, individuals with navigational capital are skilled at connecting dots, communities, and resources in ways that allow them to persist and succeed in their endeavors—even when their route is more circuitous than that of others, or when fear and doubt are naggingly present (Solórzano & Villalpando, 1998).

Linguistic Capital

When I first began my career, I remember calling home one morning to talk to my sister about my niece. She was starting college as I was finishing up with my doctorate. I recall sharing what I learned about financial aid forms and talking through the intricacies of the process. A couple hours later, I met with my supervisor and discussed my plans for supporting our graduate students in the division. That afternoon, I would deliver an engaging workshop to first-generation high school students who had been awarded full academic scholarships to the university. I would tell them about my own journey and how my peer network had influenced me along the way. They asked questions about whether I was scared to leave home and my community, and I said yes—but I did it because I knew it was the best thing for me and that it would allow me to both give back and pay it forward. I felt completely at home talking to them. I called my best friend as I headed home to tell her about how busy my day had been and to laugh with her about things that only she and I would understand. It was, and still is, typical for me to have to speak in multiple styles of speaking to be authentically heard. For each of those interactions, my tone and diction would change as necessary to connect with the intended audience. Looking back, I recognize that my ability to cater my message so that it would be relevant to each person or group was a skill, but at the time, I remember very carefully structuring my conversation in professional settings to avoid being discovered as an outsider. Even when I was promoted over the years, I often wondered if the time would come when I would not know the right things to say and give away the fact that I was not one of "them."

I came to understand how my ability to be in a space and always be me was a form of capital and, in fact, a true dividend of the totality of my experiences in blending in without losing myself in the process.

Linguistic capital undergirds the capacity of individuals to immerse themselves in environments or institutions and uses the "intellectual and social skills attained through communication experiences in more than one language and/or style" (Yosso, 2005, p. 78). It involves strong critical thinking and code switching, which is the ability to shift languages or speech styles to communicate and develops largely from racial, ethnic, or cultural experiences. Linguistic capital affords many first-generation professionals who feel like imposters the opportunity to still engage and broker in a variety of manners and settings, thereby increasing networks and strengthening their wayfinding and story-telling abilities in academic and other environments (Pérez & Taylor, 2016; Sáenz et al., 2017). A strong acumen in shifting language and ways of speaking emerges, and for many first-generation profession-als, these skills of cross-cultural awareness, bilingualism, or language style are engaged as an asset as they grow, thrive, and progress toward degree attainment and beyond. Linguistic capital also shows up as one member of a group learns information and then shares or expands upon it with members of their community with whom needed infor-mation had not been previously communicated or shared in a rel-evant frame. For instance, one first-generation student may use their linguistic capital to translate what is being said in a presentation to their parents who are not fluent in the language used, while another may use it for storytelling in the form of culturally relevant music, poetry, drawings, or other forms of artistic creation.

Familial Capital

"She's a doctor now! We did that!" My sister proudly proclaimed after my graduation ceremony. I agreed with her then, and I still do. *We* did it. My family metaphorically held my hand and guarded me along the way. They had no clue what positions I would go on to hold with a doctorate degree in educational policy and leadership, but they knew that they were proud of me and screamed and clapped excitedly for me during my graduation ceremony. Since the day I earned my first degree, they knew I would normalize a new pathway of success for my younger siblings, nieces, and nephews. They knew that they were simply cheering me on as the first leg of our family's relay. I was first, but I have come to recognize how much they did to get me to each stage of the race. I realized just how much my being first meant when my niece was asked what she would do after graduation—and she quickly and proudly responded that she was heading to college. She said it almost as though it was a silly question for someone to ask her. After all, she had always been taught that college was the goal. It had taken one generation for those who came later to know the way forward. Even when self-doubt crept in and I felt unready to begin a new career, my family's love and support helped keep me firmly grounded. Were it not for how they supported me during my journey, I likely would not have truly understood how important it was for me to do the same when my brother and my niece each started their own paths in higher education. To this day, when I feel out of place, I look back at the cards I received over the years from my family, and they bring me a sense of peace. I draw strength from my loved ones' faith and pride in me. Although I may feel like an imposter at times, I know—without question—that my family sees me as nothing of the sort, and that makes all the difference.

Familial capital refers to the nurturing and support received from one's family and is often held by first-generation professionals as being pivotal to their success. This capital not only provides moral encouragement but is a sense of pride and fuel for one's journey, buffering against uncertainty and insecurity (Sáenz et al., 2018; Yosso, 2005). A strong engagement of family capital equips students to better deal with challenging situations and extends far beyond those individuals living within a household or a shared bloodline. Familial capital also connects to the larger community and creates a deeper sense of cultural awareness as history is developed and shared (Sáenz et al., 2018). It helps students understand that support can exist in many ways. It can be seen when a family member shares on social media how proud they are of a loved one for getting into or attending a university. It's there when someone receives a note of congratulations from a neighbor and posts it on their bedroom mirror as a constant reminder that others are championing their success. It shows in small or large financial gifts received from family and friends or in the text message received from a cousin on the first day of work or classes, and it helps to quell any feelings of doubt or inadequacy.

Social Capital

"Do y'all mind if I sit here?" The young Black woman in the group smiled back at me and motioned for me to join her at a table in the Black cultural center at The Ohio State University. It would come to be one of the single most important interactions of my graduate school career, as it introduced me to the Black Graduate and Professional Student Caucus. From the caucus, I would gain mentors, sponsors, friends, study mates, financial aid leads, summer job opportunities, and a plethora of other sources of capital. I would come to learn more about myself as a Black woman navigating a multitude of spaces and would find a community in which I could be me—with no thoughts of what it meant to be an "other." There were numerous other first-generation professionals as well as peers representing the third generation of college graduates in their families. There were mentors who had been a part of the campus community for more than 30 years and scholars who helped us write grants and submit papers for publication. It was truly an environment of brilliance and excellence, yet it lacked the pressure of judgment that I often believed existed in other spaces. It was a social network that allowed me to set aside nagging notions of imposterism. I felt I could be the sum of all my parts—freely and without fears of being unmasked.

Social capital refers to the entirety of a support network: friends, peers, mentors, sponsors, community members and resources, and other social contacts who facilitate access to college and help individuals navigate other institutions (Stanton-Salazar, 2001; Yosso, 2005). For first-generation professionals, social capital can be one family telling another about their student's experiences completing financial aid forms or applying for college scholarships. It can be sharing interview tips or telling a peer what they should wear for a job interview, as it may be the first for that person. Peer mentoring shares social capital by connecting students to each other, and it creates space for knowledge to be exchanged and passed down through cohorts. It can be observed in a social media group that appeals to a specific identity—such as Black women in higher education, college athletes, commuter students or African American living-learning communities—as a means of sharing support and resources. Social capital has long been widely engaged by communities of color who have unified to navigate the academy and beyond, to increase agency, and to provide critical emotional and pragmatic support. Strong social capital can be shared with one's social network, as well as paid forward later as individuals and communities work to reduce stigma and eliminate barriers.

Resistant Capital

"Tell me a word that starts with the letter *d* that resonates with you." Without thinking twice, I responded: "defiant." This was during an ice breaker at a professional conference about a year ago, and I could immediately see my small group's eyebrows raise with curiosity. I went on to explain how, for years, imposter syndrome had played a role in my life and had led me to overachieve for fear of being exposed as a fraud. I further explained that, however, in recent years, I made the conscious decision to be influenced not by doubt but by defiance. I recalled how a sorority sister had given me the poem "Phenomenal Woman" by Maya Angelou during my sophomore year and had me recite it to her whenever I saw her. To this day, I can tell you every single word, and I carry it with me in my heart. My entire life, I worked hard to achieve my goals, to help others, and to be a "mirror" for those who needed one. I have constantly worked to overcome barriers placed in my path and find ways to remove them for others. I finally decided then, even when I had insecurities, I would honor the fact that I am not by any means a fraud. I realized my worries of being unmasked were unfounded and unhelpful; I realized that I needed to *feel* as confident as I was believed to be by others. I chose to resist feeling as though I did not belong in spaces that I had worked hard to occupy. I resisted the urge to see myself as less-than—by choosing defiance over doubt.

For first-generation professionals and other underserved groups, *resistant capital* is often leveraged to challenge oppression; in other words, individuals choose to carry on despite inequality and institutional barriers to their success, and they apply the "knowledge and skills fostered through oppositional behavior that challenges inequality" (Yosso, 2005, p. 80). Resistant capital exists in messages passed down from family and learned through community or personal interactions. These messages bolster individuals' sense of self by reinforcing that individuals are good enough—despite systemic counter-messaging and shortsighted thematizing that portrays underserved communities as less-than. Resistant capital serves as a constant reminder to be the best version of one's self despite this, challenging the status quo and the structural nature of oppression (Yosso, 2005). In notions that hope itself is not a strategy, it is inherent: Hard work and the ability to outmaneuver structural barriers, covert impediments, and oppressive societal messages are what enables a person to thrive, succeed, and create a legacy of excellence for others to emulate.

Intersecting forms of community cultural wealth express the crux of resistant capital itself, which is that collective resources are not "mutually exclusive or static, but rather dynamic processes that build on one another as part of community cultural wealth" (Yosso, 2005, p. 77). The accumulation of shared resources honors parents, family members, and ancestors who sacrificed much to create pathways and opportunities for younger generations they themselves never had. Resistant capital shows up as a deviation from what the majority group considers the norm or typical way of being or advancing; for many marginalized persons or groups, it can be communicated loudly and proudly in their art, clothing, academic coursework, marches and demonstrations, television shows, and so on. Examples of resistant capital can also be seen in hip-hop lyrics and in social media campaigns; through direct and bold messaging such as "Black Lives Matter," "Black Girl Magic," and "women belong in all places where decisions are being made"; and on T-shirts that read "proud child of an immigrant," "little girls with dreams become women with vision," or "first-generation and proud to lead the way." Essentially, resistant culture serves to frame, center, embody, and vocalize the views and experiences of underserved communities. It emerges as a useful tool for many first-generation professionals as they leverage nontraditional forms of wealth in their navigation of various personal and professional contexts, including institutions of higher education.

Conclusion

"We don't have to do it all alone. We were never meant to." —Brené Brown, *Rising Strong*

Without question, the framework of community cultural wealth helped me better understand the strengths, history, and experiences of many marginalized persons—as well as myself. Today, I still navigate spaces as a first-generation college graduate, and occasionally I still experience bouts of imposter syndrome. I maneuver these experiences knowing that what I offer professionally and personally is due to the positioning and leveraging of my own cultural capital. I navigate these challenges as a Black woman. I always will. And if given the choice, I would choose the same journey again. I don't see my identities as marginalized; I see them as magnified, as each has helped me navigate a variety of setting and scenarios. I embrace the opportunities that come with "leading from the front." Being first means having the opportunity to explore unchartered territory as well as having an experience and narrative to share with those taking the voyage after you. I did not do it alone; I have an extended community of first-generation peers and colleagues with whom I share many commonalities.

There has been a depth of cultural convergence along the way, and many of my colleagues have acknowledged their experiences with imposter syndrome, too. I also recognize that I have long possessed the tools, social strategies, cultural competencies, and inner resources needed to excel and thrive, even when doubts and fears of fraudulence creep in. Ultimately, what I may not have sported in traditional resources, social capital, or financial assets, I made up for in agency, which was pivotal to how I showed up for, to, and with others—and myself. I am a better and more culturally responsive educator because of my journey and my understanding of the need to eliminate a deficit mindset for supporting marginalized groups and persons and the need to reframe our policies, practices, and procedures to that end. I was never deficient; my assets and wealth were just different. When I learned to focus on what I am instead of what I am not, my worldview changed. An understanding of community cultural wealth helped me remove my mask and embrace the reality that I am not an imposter: I have been able to move forward professionally and personally because of what I have—not what I lack.

That is wealth indeed.

Questions for Reflection

Self-reflection allows you to appreciate your own story, that of numerous colleagues, and the students and staff you will support over time, many of whom will struggle with imposter syndrome at some point. Self-reflection implores us to eliminate notions of social stratification. It compels us to understand the importance of our own and others' communities, families, networks, and actions, as well as the spoken and unspoken words that can shape institutions over time. It is about challenging and successfully navigating the status quo. It is the opportunity to un-privilege systems and traditional ways of knowing and doing with the purpose of strengthening frameworks and being a mirror, sounding board, and strategist for those around us and those yet to make their way to or through the academy and beyond. It is about taking off the mask of imposterism and embracing the stories that have framed success for so many first-generation professionals; it is about recognizing how many have used their strengths to find their way and press forward while overcoming structural barriers.

Imposter syndrome is the product of false perceptions of inadequacy; community cultural wealth affords us an opportunity to view the impact of our strengths in combatting it. We must reflect on and consider our experiences as we navigate academic and professional settings. It is also important to contemplate how we can better support first-generation staff and students who may encounter imposter syndrome as they navigate compounding and conflicting social identities; we must show them how they have already engaged their resources and assets to achieve.

Ask yourself:

- In terms of your experiences with imposter syndrome, where and how did it begin? How has it shown itself along your journey?
- What messages did you speak to yourself? Has your narrative shifted over time?
- In moving forward professionally and personally, how do you overcome feelings of inadequacy and skepticism? How do you embrace the depths of who you are by drawing on your strengths, resources, and network of support? In what ways have you navigated imposter syndrome by engaging elements of community cultural wealth (aspirational, linguistic, familial, social, navigational, and/or resistant capital)?
- How have compounding factors (e.g., imposter syndrome, upbringing, microaggressions, bias) compelled you to engage aspects of community cultural wealth? What are specific instances where it helped you to overcome obstacles or barriers?
- Which facets of community cultural wealth did you learn from your parents, guardians, or family members? From your peers? From your community?
- Which facet of community cultural wealth best informs your role as a professional or a student? How do you demonstrate this capital to others?
- In terms of supporting first-generation professionals, how can you use the framework of community cultural wealth to eliminate structural and institutional barriers for marginalized students and groups?

- Think about your own assumptions regarding first-generation professionals. How do they inform your interactions and engagement with this community of students and staff? How might you shift resources or your approach to leverage their strengths, skills, and experiences?
- In what other contexts might you use or apply Yosso's framework to increase your understanding, outreach, and impact?

References

Bernard, N. S., Dollinger, S. J., & Ramaniah, N. V. (2002). Applying the big five personality factors to the impostor phenomenon. *Journal of Personality Assessment, 78*(2), 321–333. https://doi.org/10.1207/S15327752JPA7802_07

Bourdieu, P. (1986). The forms of capital. In J. Richardson (Ed.), *Handbook of theory and research for the sociology of education* (pp. 241–258). Greenwood. https://www.marxists.org/reference/subject/philosophy/works/fr/bourdieu-forms-capital.htm

Bourdieu, P., & Passeron, J. C. (1979). *The inheritors: French students and their relation to culture.* University of Chicago Press.

Bui, K. V. T. (2002). First-generation college students at a four-year university: Background characteristics, reasons for pursuing higher education, and first-year experiences. *College Student Journal, 36*(1), 3–11.

Bussotti, C. (1990). The impostor phenomenon: Family roles and environment. *Dissertation Abstracts International, 51*, 4041–4042(B).

Chakraverty, D. (2019). Impostor phenomenon in STEM: Occurrence, attribution, and identity. *Studies in Graduate and Postdoctoral Education, 10*(1), 2–20. https://doi.org/10.1108/SGPE-D-18-00014

Cisco, J. (2020). Using academic skill set interventions to reduce impostor phenomenon feelings in postgraduate students. *Journal of Further and Higher Education, 44*(3), 423–437. https://doi.org/10.1080/0309877X.2018.1564023

Clance, P. R. (1985). *The impostor phenomenon: When success makes you feel like a fake.* Peachtree.

Clance, P. R., & Imes, S. A. (1978). The imposter phenomenon in high achieving women: Dynamics and therapeutic intervention. *Psychotherapy: Theory, Research & Practice, 15*(3), 241–247. https://doi.org/10.1037/h0086006

Clance, P. R., & O'Toole, M. A. (1988). The impostor phenomenon: An internal barrier to empowerment and achievement. *Women and Therapy, 6*(3), 51–64. https://doi.org/10.1300/J015V06N03_05

Cokley, K., McClain, S., Enciso, A., & Martinez, M. (2013). An examination of the impact of minority status stress and impostor feelings on the mental health of diverse ethnic minority college students. *Journal of Multicultural Counseling and Development, 41*(2), 82–95. https://doi.org/10.1002/j.2161-1912.2013.00029.x

Cope-Watson, G. & Betts, A. S. (2010). Confronting otherness: An e-conversation between doctoral students living with the imposter syndrome. *Canadian Journal for New Scholars in Education, 3*(1), 1–13.

Craddock, S., Birnbaum, M., Rodriguez, K., Cobb, C., & Zeeh, S. (2011). Doctoral students and the impostor phenomenon: Am I smart enough to be here? *Journal of Student Affairs Research and Practice, 48*(4), 429–442. https://doi.org/10.2202/1949-6605.6321

Crenshaw, K. (1991). Mapping the margins: Intersectionality, identity politics, and violence against women of color. *Stanford Law Review, 43*(6), 1241–1299. https://doi.org/10.2307/1229039

Dika, S., & D'Amico, M. (2016). Early experiences and integration in the persistence of first-generation college students in STEM and non-STEM majors. *Journal of Research in Science Teaching, 53*(3), 368–383. https://doi.org/10.1002/tea.21301

Ewing, K. M., Richardson, T. Q., James-Myers, L., & Russell, R. K. (1996). The relationship between racial identity attitudes, worldview, and African American graduate students' experience of the imposter phenomenon. *The Journal of Black Psychology, 22*, 53–66. https://doi.org/10.1177/00957984960221005

Gándara, P. C. (1995). *Over the ivy walls: The educational mobility of low-income Chicanos.* State University of New York Press.

Gardner, S., & Holley, K. (2011). "Those invisible barriers are real": The progression of first-generation students through doctoral education. *Equity & Excellence in Education, 44*, 77–92. https://doi.org/10.1080/10665684.2011.529791

Gibson-Beverly, G., & Schwartz, J. P. (2008). Attachment, entitlement, and the impostor phenomenon in female graduate students. *Journal of College Counseling, 11*(2), 119–132. https://doi.org/10.1002/j.2161-1882.2008.tb00029.x

Gravois, J. (2007, November 9). You're not fooling anyone. *The Chronicle of Higher Education.* https://www.chronicle.com/article/youre-not-fooling-anyone

Harvey, J. C., & Katz, C. (1985). *If I'm so successful, why do I feel like a fake? The impostor phenomenon.* St. Martin's Press.

Hurtado, S. (1994). The institutional climate for talented Latino students. *Research in Higher Education, 35*(1), 21–41. https://www.jstor.org/stable/40196058

Hutchins, H. M. (2015). Outing the imposter: A study exploring imposter phenomenon among higher education faculty. *New Horizons in Adult Education and Human Resource Development, 27*, 3–12. https://doi.org/10.1002/nha3.20098

Ishitani, T. T. (2006). Studying attrition and degree completion behavior among first-generation college students in the United States. *Journal of Higher Education, 77*(5), 861–885. https://doi.org/10.1080/00221546.2006.11778947

Knights, D., & Clarke, C. A. (2014). It's a bittersweet symphony, this life: Fragile academic selves and insecure identities at work. *Organization Studies, 35*(3), 335–357. https://doi.org/10.1177/0170840613508396

Kumar, S., & Jagacinski, C. M. (2006). Imposters have goals too: The imposter phenomenon and its relationship to achievement goal theory. *Personality and Individual Differences, 40*, 147–157. https://doi.org/10.1016/j.paid.2005.05.014

Martinez, J. A., Sher, K. J., Krull, J. L., & Wood, P. K. (2009). Blue-collar scholars? Mediators and moderators of university attrition in first-generation college students. *Journal of College Student Development, 50*, 87–103. https://doi.org/10.1353/csd.0.0053

Mattie, C., Gietzen, J., Davis, S., & Prata, J. (2008). The imposter phenomenon: Self-assessment and competency to perform as a physician assistant in the United States. *The Journal of Physician Assistant Education, 19*(1), 5–12. https://doi.org/10.1097/01367895-200819010-00002

McClain, S., Beasley, S. T., Jones, B., Awosogba, O., Jackson, S., & Cokley, K. (2016). An examination of the impact of racial and ethnic identity, impostor feelings, and minority status stress on the mental health of Black college students. *Journal of Multicultural Counseling and Development, 44*(2), 101–117. https://doi.org/10.1002/jmcd.12040

Naumann, W. C., Bandalos, D., & Gutkin, T. B. (2003). Identifying variables that predict college success for first-generation college students. *Journal of College Admission, 181*, 4.

Pérez, I. I., & Taylor, K. B. (2016). *Cultivando logradores*: Nurturing and sustaining Latino male success in higher education. *Journal of Diversity in Higher Education, 9*(1), 1–19. https://doi.org/10.1037/a0039145

Perna, L. (2006). Studying college access and choice: A proposed conceptual model. In J. C. Smart (Ed.), *Higher education: Handbook of theory and research* (Vol. 21, pp. 99–157). Springer.

Peteet, B., Montgomery, L., & Weekes, J. (2015). Predictors of imposter phenomenon among talented ethnic minority undergraduate students. *The Journal of Negro Education, 84*, 175–186. https://doi.org/10.7709/jnegroeducation.84.2.0175

Sáenz, V. B., de las Mercédez, C., Rodriguez, S. G., & García-Louis, C. (2017). Latino men and their fathers: Exploring how Community Cultural Wealth influences their community college success. *Association of Mexican American Educators Journal, 11*(2), 89–110. https://doi.org/10.24974/amae.11.2.351

Sáenz, V. B., García-Louis, C., Drake, A. P., & Guida, T. (2018). Leveraging their family capital: How Latino males successfully navigate the community college. *Community College Review, 46*(1), 40–61. https://doi.org/10.1177/0091552117743567

Settles, I. H., Cortina, L. M., Buchanan, N. T., & Miner, K. N. (2013). Derogation, discrimination, and (dis)satisfaction with jobs in science: A gendered analysis. *Psychology of Women Quarterly, 37*(2), 179–191. https://doi.org/10.1177/0361684312468727

Solórzano, D., Ceja, M., & Yosso, T. (2000). Critical race theory, racial microaggressions, and campus racial climate: The experiences of African American college students. *The Journal of Negro Education, 69*(1/2), 60–73. https://www.jstor.org/stable/2696265

Solórzano, D., & Villalpando, O. (1995). Critical race theory, marginality, and the experience of students of color in higher education. In C. A. Torres & T. Mitchell (Eds.), *Sociology of education: Emerging perspectives* (pp. 211–224). State University of New York Press.

Stanton-Salazar, R. D. (2001). *Manufacturing hope and despair: The school and kin support networks of U.S.-Mexican youth.* Teachers College Press.

Terenzini, P. T., Springer, L., Yaeger, P., Pascarella, E. T., & Nora, A. (1996). First-generation college students: Characteristics, experiences and cognitive development. *Research in Higher Education, 37*(1), 1–22. https://doi.org/10.1007/BF01680039

Thompson, T., Foreman, P., & Martin, F. (2000). Impostor fears and perfectionistic concern over mistakes. *Personality and Individual Differences, 29*(4), 692–647. https://doi.org/10.1016/S0191-8869(99)00218-4

Topping, M. E. H. (1983). *The impostor phenomenon: A study of its construct and incidence in university faculty members* [Unpublished doctoral dissertation]. University of South Florida.

Trefts, S. (2019). *The imposter phenomenon in female, first-generation STEM majors* (Publication No. 13865876) [Doctoral Dissertation, Californian Lutheran University]. ProQuest Dissertations and Theses Global.

Walpole, M. (2003). Socioeconomic status and college: How SES affects college experiences and outcomes. *The Review of Higher Education, 27*(1), 45–73. https://doi.org/10.1353/rhe.2003.0044

Yosso, T. J. (2005). Whose culture has capital? A critical race theory discussion of community cultural wealth. *Race Ethnicity and Education, 8*(1), 69–91. https://doi.org/10.1080/1361332052000341006

3

Navigating Bureaucracy and Politics

WILLIE BANKS

Bureaucracy and politics are part of most professional careers. First-generation professionals, in particular, may struggle with the nuances of hierarchical structures and power dynamics. The term *navigational capital* refers to the abilities and skills to manuever "social institutions," which include colleges and universities (Yosso, 2005). Turner (1997) defined *social institutions* as "a complex of positions, roles, norms, and values lodged in particular types of social structures and organising relatively stable patterns of human activity with respect to fundamental problems in producing life-sustaining resources, in reproducing individuals, and in sustaining viable societal structures within a given environment" (p. 6). This chapter focuses on strategies for first-generation professionals to gain and utilize navigational capital in higher education settings.

The ability to navigate bureaucracy and politics prepares first-generation professionals to thrive in environments that may not be supportive—or that are outright hostile. Bolman and Deal (2017) presented four frames through which most organizations can be viewed. The first frame identified is structural, which is focused on tasks, strategy, and metrics within an organization. The human resources frame focuses on the people of the organization and their needs to be successful within their positions. The political frame focuses on individuals and groups within the organzaiton and the competion for power or resources. The final frame identified is symbolic, which addresses peoples' needs for a sense of purpose or meaning in their work. The frames provide insight into the values, culture, and concepts of an organization. Individuals typically identify a preference for one or two frames in their approach to their work. First-generation professionals, especially in middle management roles, are encouraged to identify preferences that will help navigate their work environment.

The political framework generally describes organizations as jungles or arenas, where there are competing interests and where conflict can arise especially with regard to resources and overall organizational direction (Bolman & Deal, 2017). An example of an organization operating within the political framework would be the University of Maryland, College Park, and its 2018 dispute with the Board of Regents of the University of Maryland System following the death of a student-athlete—and the ensuing power struggle between the two entities (Stripling, 2018). The Board of Regents wanted to retain the football coach; the university president defied the regents and fired the coach. A true power struggle, this dispute between the president and the Board of Regents played out in the national press.

Politics

First-generation professionals in positions of authority have a unique opportunity to use their experiences as first-generation students to influence change. But for some of these professionals, working in politicized settings in higher education can trigger anxiety and even cause them to question their abilities (Terry & Fobia, 2019).

Although there exists a significant amount of literature on first-generation college students and their transition and adjustment into higher education (Pascarella et al., 2004; Terry & Fobia, 2019), only limited research focuses on first-generation professionals in work settings. In Terry and Fobia's (2019) research, which focused on first-generation professionals in government agencies, the authors asserted that "similar to college and university campuses, white-collar workplace environments also tend to be populated by middle- to upper-SES [socio economic status] background employees (and thereby middle- to upper-SES values). It follows that first-generation professionals (who might also have been the first in their family to attend college) might experience similar challenges of adjustment to the workplace environment" (p. 3).

Many first-generation professionals may even feel the effects of imposter syndrome (see Chapter 2); they may have dealt with feelings of inadequacy, but transitions into new roles as managers and executives can thrust first-generation professionals into unchartered territory. For many, their success as student affairs professionals relies on their ability to navigate arenas they are not familiar with or that may not be the most affirming.

Some professionals actively sidestep politics within the context of work, but the reality is that such avoidance is neither sustainable nor accurate. One lens to consider is how politics can be used for the greater good and the advancement not only of personal interests but also of larger, community-focused goals. Bolman and Deal (2017) offered examples of the political framework as a necessary lens for competition of resources and excellence. Additionally, these authors stated that "goals, structure, and policies emerge from an ongoing process of bargaining and negotiation among major interest groups" (p. 199). For instance, during my tenure as a vice president for student affairs, many of the policies, programs, or initiatives instituted on campus have emerged from discussions between offices and units across the university and not strictly from within a student affairs department. Theoretically, someone could embark on instituting goals or policies from within their own unit, without consulting others; however, in practical terms, the odds of those goals succeeding decrease without buy-in from other units.

Simply put: Politics exist in almost every situation and at times are unavoidable. First-generation professionals make decisions on how in the workplace to present themselves, which could include, wardrobe, hair, and even language choices—all political decisions. There are unwritten rules not set by any professional but set by the organization's history and culture. These uspoken rules are similar to the "hidden curriculum" that has typically been discussed within the context of K–12 education environments; however, they can be applied to higher education (Margolis et al., 2001). Margolis et al. (2001) further discussed the concept by explaining "the hidden curriculum may be intentionally hidden in plain sight, precisely so that it will remain undetected. Much of the built environment, issues related to the body, the statuses of disciplines, and the ranks of higher education institutions are hiding in plain sight. . . . As another important story in Western cultures teaches, curricula can be hidden by general social agreement not to see" (p. 2). For the first-generation professional, navigating the hidden curriculum—the unspoken rules—can be daunting; and if you are not privy to the hidden curriculum, how can you be successful?

Within the work environment, instead of actively avoiding politics, professionals could embrace a political framework and look to capitalize on the benefits of engaging with a political organization. This approach can be uncomfortable; however, these politicized workplace spaces are no different than the spaces first-generation professionals encountered as first-generation college students. Many first-generation college students remember the first time they set foot on their campus and how they tried to navigate the complex bureaucracy. For many college students, they had to figure out the purpose of certain offices, which individuals to go to for assistance, and/or how to navigate policies or procedures. Those experiences shaped first-generation professionals, allowing them to understand and appreciate the realities of being a first-generation college student. The challenges faced in college prepared first-generation professionals for the often unsettling world of higher education. It is important for first-generation professionals to embrace their experiences and use them to guide their work with students.

During my first tenure as a vice president for student affairs, I frequently retold my story of arriving on my undergraduate campus as a first-generation student. I shared my experiences of trying to figure out how to navigate the bureaucracy and find my way around campus. One antidote I shared involved me arriving on campus for my freshman year of college with a full-tuition scholarship. A few weeks into the fall quarter I received a bill from the bursar's office requesting payment for room and board. I had assumed my scholarship covered room and board costs. When I received this bill, I had to go to several offices to fully understand what my scholarship covered and did not cover. I quickly had to find on-campus jobs, and my parents had to take out a loan to help pay for my education. This story helped me connect with a wide variety of students, faculty, and staff. I was able to give a tangible example of the struggle many first-generation students face. This story also provided an opportunity to discuss how my vision and decision-making process for the Division of Student Affairs had been shaped by my experiences as a first-generation college student. Sharing a personal story and connecting it with the present-day realities of students and staff can help build relationships and advance the mission of your work.

Navigational Capital

The community cultural wealth model (Yosso, 2005; see Chapter 2 for more information) helps first-generation professionals think about their work from a strengths-based approach and "acknowledges individual agency within institutional constraints, but it also connects to social networks that facilitate community navigation through places and spaces including schools, the job market, and the health care and judicial systems" (p. 80). First-generation professionals are already equipped to navigate these spaces, using the resiliency they developed to survive college. As Yosso (2005) pointed out, communities of color are culturally rich and have prepared community members to be resilient and successful in navigating social institutions, including educational institutions. Much like communities of color, first-generation professionals are just as prepared and flexible to work successfully within these new spaces.

First-generation professionals should consider how to find supportive environments within their institutions—how to spot allies who can provide guidance and information on how to navigate the bureaucracy. Many first-generation professionals have thrived in situations where their authority is questioned or where they are working with or for individuals who seek to undermine their presence within their organizations. Using the reframing technique (Bolman & Deal, 2017), which is described as finding opportunities and options within complicated and troubled organizations, first-generation professionals can take an uncomfortable situation and make it into an opportunity to use to their advantage. For example, if a coworker or a manager questioned your work, you could ask more specific questions and attempt to get more clarity on expectations. Asking questions in this situation would demonstrate your ability to pivot at a moment's notice and to take feedback. Viewing this situation as a learning opportunity rather than a punitive matter may yield greater understanding of the organization's culture.

In 2015, when I was vice president for student affairs, the Black Lives Matter movement afforded me several openings to reframe tough conversations on race and equity. I recounted my experiences as being a queer, multiracial, African American, Asian American, first-generation student navigating the complexities of higher education. In my undergraduate career, my success was partially due to being able to find a community. As vice president for student affairs, I recognized that our institution needed to find ways to create community and spaces for marginalized communities. I was able use my story to transform a conversation about race and equity into real action—with the creation of several centers for women as well as LGBTQIA+, international, and multicultural students.

More than a few first-generation professionals have benefited from mentorships. Many of us rely on mentors, colleagues, and outside networks to figure out how to successfully navigate the politics of our campus. I rely on a number of colleagues and friends to help me investigate a position and to consider the culture and environment of an institution. Relying on others for wise counsel and tips to navigate these positions and situations is extremely important, because these individuals can offer specific feedback on common matters. Often, seeking feedback from mentors outside of the institution allows for unbiased feedback. I depend on a community of other vice president colleagues to discuss various political situations within my division as well as possible solutions. To better understand and navigate situations, you should seek colleagues who ask tough questions and give unfiltered feedback.

It is important to approach the political environment in a similar way as starting college. The following are some helpful tips for first-generation professionals seeking to navigate new and unfamiliar spaces, such as meetings with external stakeholders (universitywide or collegewide committees, donors, etc.) or with faculty colleagues (academic senate, etc.). Many first-generation professionals in middle management may be attending these types of meetings for the first time, and many mid-level professionals may be encountering faculty government for the first time. These structures are filled with influence, institutional decision making, and networking opportunities.

In these meetings, so much of what is not said is just as important as what is said. A colleague of mine offered great advice: "Go on a LOL tour, which stands for listening, observing, and learning." The LOL tour is not a unique concept; leaders in many sectors have spoken about its effectiveness when professionals are transitioning into new roles (Eikenberry, 2011; Faughnan, 2020; Kenny, 2019). While relatively simple, this process allows someone in a new position to meet a variety of colleagues and stakeholders and to learn about the nuances of a new institution. The LOL tour introduces you to the stakeholders: What agenda does each person have? How can you leverage it to succeed in your new environment?

Politics is based on relationships (Bolman & Deal, 2017). For first-generation professionals, understanding the political landscape takes patience and a keen understanding of people, organizational culture, and relationships. It also takes knowing various individuals throughout the organization. When many first-generation students attended college, their experiences in navigating higher education were based on trial and error. They had to figure out the offices, people, and culture of the institution. Much like attending college for the first time, first-generation professionals in mid-manager and senior-level roles must approach their work with a spirit of exploration and learning.

Listen

Listening can be a powerful tool to understand the culture of an organization. Llopis (2013) identified six ways listening can make better leaders.

1. Show that you care: Demonstrate to employees that you see them as more than just a worker. Employees want leaders who can show that they care about them and the larger organization.

2. Engage yourself: Engage with your employees in meaningful ways. Go beyond the surface and learn what drives the organization and its employees.
3. Be empathetic: Demonstrate an understanding of your employees and the organization. At the same time, be approachable and engage in emotional interactions. Llopis (2013) noted, "Empathy is a powerful display of listening" (para 13).
4. Don't judge others: Don't criticize others; instead learn from others. Be open to new ways of learning and doing.
5. Be mindful: Understand and digest your surroundings. Be mindful of what is—and is not—said.
6. Don't interrupt: Be a compassionate leader who practices two-way communication, allowing others to finish their thoughts and being patient.

Llopis (2013) pointed out that "listening goes well beyond being quiet and giving someone your full attention. It requires you to be aware of body language, facial expressions, mood, and natural behavioral tendencies. Listening should be a full-time job when you consider the uncertainty embedded in the workplace and the ongoing changes taking place" (para. 2).

Sometimes what is not said in meetings is just as important as what is said. Listen to the voices in the room and take note of who is speaking and who is not—this may reveal power dynamics within the organizational culture. It will also shed light on the priorities of the unit or institution. Certain themes may emerge; conversations can reveal priorities, potential land mines, and coalitions that must be formed to advance directives. Pay attention to where information is coming from and what information is shared; this may indicate who can be trusted with information and who cannot.

During my own LOL tour in my first position as a vice president for student affairs, I attended a universitywide president's council meeting comprised of campus leadership from across the university.

During the meeting I heard from various stakeholders on the progress of certain projects; I also learned about priorities from the divisions represented, including student affairs, university advancement, academic affairs, and community engagement. This meeting helped me to understand not only the priorities of the divisions but those of the university. Many of the items discussed intersected with multiple divisions from across the university.

Observe

Much like listening, observation of the surroundings and the complex bureaucracies of higher education is required (Clancey, 2006). Denison and Spreitzer (1991) asserted that to "understand or change an organization, a researcher or change agent must first examine the linkages between underlying values, organizational structures, and individual meaning" (p. 2). First-generation professionals should take advantage of all opportunities to observe: Attend meetings and social events sponsored by the institution; go to athletic events and community functions; and always take the opportunity to visit offices or units. Note where colleagues sit during meetings. Pay attention to the location of buildings and offices. Many times, the location of offices can shed light on power structures and hierarchy. Often, the power structure of an organization is physically near the president or chancellor. On many campuses, the administration building serves as the de facto center of power, and the offices within the building can indicate where power lies. It is not uncommon to hear of infighting or jockeying by leaders to secure and occupy office space near the center of power. Observing the placement of offices can help you understand where power may or may not exist.

Observing various groups in their own settings can yield valuable information on the organizational culture to first-generation professionals. They should take note of how the offices are designed. What is the condition of the furniture? Is this an indication of the institution's priorities? During meetings, where do people sit? Is the leader sitting at the head of the table, or is the leader seated among staff members? What is the tone and tenor of the meeting? Is there a relaxed atmosphere or a more formal structure to the meetings? All of these questions can lead to a general assessment about the organization's culture. Of course, beyond observing these spaces, you must listen to and consult with others to best assess the organizational culture.

Learn

In my first year in my first position as a vice president for student affairs, I utilized the LOL tour. Typically, many organizations will provide an onboarding experience that allows for someone to take a LOL tour. During my first such tour, I interacted with many offices and individuals from across campus—athletics, faculty senate president, finance and administration, student government, the provost— as well as members of my own organization. The tour gave me a clearer picture of how staff experienced certain issues, as well as how colleagues and senior leaders viewed the division. I listened to stories of the division's achievements—as well as its shortcomings. I was able to observe how individuals interacted with me and learned more about the organizational culture and history. The LOL tour helped me devise a direction and plan for the division, which included new priorities, the creation of departments, and a reorganization of the structure. My plan was informed by listening, observing, and learning from others and understanding the culture of the organization. I presented the plan to the president, which helped the division secure resources to implement the new initiatives.

Ultimately, to better understand campus power and politics, first-generation professionals should combine the information gleaned from listening and observing. For those professionals in new positions or in a new institution, the insights gained from the LOL tour can be particularly beneficial.

Build Coalitions

One of the most important tips for first-generation professionals is to build a coalition. A coalition is characterized as an "interacting group of individuals, deliberately constructed, independent of the formal structure, lacking its own internal formal structure, consisting of mutually perceived membership, issue oriented, focused on a goal or goals external to the coalition, and requiring concerted member action" (Stevenson et al., 1985, p. 261). Coalitions are key to the success of first-generation professionals. It is highly unlikely for the work occurring within individual offices to not intersect with other units within the larger organization. Coalitions can help secure resources, advance directives, and provide additional support for new or ongoing initiatives. Approaching the work from a perspective of a collective "we" instead of a singular "I" speaks to the importance and the power of working together. Further, recent, pressing issues in higher education (making tuition affordable, combatting racism, ensuring access, allocating resources, etc.) require the collective work of coalitions to make meaningful change.

As a first-generation professional, you must understand that your work requires vision and direction; it also calls for the ability to work collaboratively with others, manage personnel and budgets, delegate assignments, and ultimately lead your unit. Success in these areas requires preparation and a game plan.

The LOL tour will offer you the chance to gather data, which will help inform and shape the direction and focus of your work. You must validate the information received—as you would with any other form of research—and that is why building a coalition can be an effective tool for navigating the political environment. Schedule time with coalition members to review the findings of your LOL tour. It is important to find those coalition members who can provide unfiltered and honest opinions about your initial findings. These coalition members should be able to provide context, as it will ultimately lead to you better understanding your working environment.

In my work as a vice president for student affairs, I had success when I had a game plan. My game plan consisted of doing research on the organization, going on a LOL tour, developing a vision/plan for the division, validating the direction with coalition members, and then presenting the vision/plan to internal and external stakeholders to build buy-in and support.

Having a solid game plan demonstrates an ability to understand the complexities of an organization and what is necessary to lead effectively. Additionally, having effective coalitions to help share and champion your mission or ideas will help move your agenda forward. The support from a wide variety of stakeholders will help you navigate the political nature of your organization.

Conclusion

First-generation professionals are uniquely situated to use their experiences as first-generation college students to succeed in navigating the complex bureaucracies of higher education. First-generation professionals through their life experiences and resilient nature are well equipped to be effective leaders. Understanding their own navigational capital (Yosso, 2005) as it relates to higher education settings, as well as Bolman and Deal's (2017) four frames, will help first-generation professionals be successful in their careers. Grasping the nature of the political framework; acknowledging the necessity to listen, observe, and learn; and building coalitions will help first-generation professionals lead higher education organizations to success.

Questions for Reflection

1. Consider your experiences as a first-generation college student and write down how you were able to navigate the institution. What assisted you through that process? What offices or people helped you understand the institution and how to succeed in it? Are there comparable people or offices that can provide that level of support to you now that you are a first-generation professional?

2. What stressors or triggers contribute to feelings of anxiousness or uncertainty in your new position? What can you do to work through those issues? What strengths do you bring to this new situation? What opportunities exist for professional development or coaching to help address these stressors or triggers?

3. On which colleagues can you rely to provide unfiltered feedback to help you in your position? Identify individuals inside and outside of the institution who can be a sounding board and can offer counsel regarding work issues. Identify work colleagues at a similar level or above who can also be in your inner circle.

4. Start building coalitions. Identify individuals or offices that would be good partners to advance the mission of your office or cause. Look for offices or individuals that share common values or missions.

5. Conduct a LOL tour with offices and colleagues. What did you hear when you were on your tour? What did you observe? What did you learn from the LOL tour? How does this information inform your leadership

and management? What does it say about the culture of your organization? What didn't you hear on your tour? What didn't you observe? What was missing?

References

Bolman, L. G., & Deal, T. E. (2017). *Reframing organizations: Artistry, choice, and leadership* (6th ed.). Wiley & Sons.

Clancey, W. J. (2006). Observation of work practices in natural settings. In K. A. Ericcson, N. Charness, P. J. Feltovich, & R. R. Hoffman (Eds.), *The Cambridge handbook of expertise and expert performance* (pp. 127–146). Cambridge University Press.

Denison, D. R., & Spreitzer, G. M. (1991). Organizational culture and organizational development: A competing values approach. *Research in Organizational Change and Development, 5*, 1–21.

Eikenberry, K. (2011). *Want to be a more effective leader? Take a listening tour.* Leadership and Learning With Kevin Eikenberry. https://blog.kevineikenberry.com/leadership-supervisory-skills/want-to-be-a-more-effective-leader-take-a-listening-tour

Faughnan, D. (2020). *How to conduct a listening tour.* Damien Faughnan: CEO Advisor & C-Suite Coach. https://damienfaughnan.com/how-to-conduct-a-listening-tour

Kenny, J. (2019, December 12). Five ways listening tours make you a more innovative leader. *Forbes.* https://www.forbes.com/sites/forbescoachescouncil/2019/12/20/five-ways-listening-tours-make-you-a-more-innovative-leader/#25ad5a925ac8

Llopis, G. (2013, May 20). Six ways effective listening can make you a better leader. *Forbes.* https://www.forbes.com/sites/glennllopis/2013/05/20/6-effective-ways-listening-can-make-you-a-better-leader/#1385029a1756

Margolis, E., Soldatenko, M., Acker, S., & Gair, M. (2001). Peekaboo: Hiding and outing the curriculum. In E. Margolis (Ed.), *The hidden curriculum in higher education* (pp. 1–19). Routledge.

Pascarella, E. T., Pierson, C. T., Wolniak, G. C., & Terenzini, P. T. (2004). First-generation college students. *The Journal of Higher Education, 75*(3), 249–284. https://doi.org/10.1080/00221546.2004.11772256

Stevenson, W. B., Pearce, J. L., & Porter, L. W. (1985, April). The concept of "coalition" in organization theory and research. *The Academy of Management Review, 10*(2), 256–268.

Stripling, J. (2018, November 9). As another head rolls at U. of Maryland, an athletics scandal turns morality play. *The Chronicle of Higher Education.* https://www.chronicle.com/article/as-another-head-rolls-at-u-of-maryland-an-athletics-scandal-turns-morality-play

Terry, R. L., & Fobia, A. C. (2019). *Qualitative research on barriers to workplace inclusion for first generation professionals* (Research Report Series, Survey Methodology #2019-03). U.S. Census Bureau. http://www.census.gov/content/dam/Census/library/working-papers/2019/adrm/rsm2019-03.pdf

Turner, J. (1997). *The institutional order: Economy, kinship, religion, polity, law, and education in evolutionary and comparative perspective.* Longman.

Yosso, T. J. (2005). Whose culture has capital? A critical race theory discussion of community cultural wealth. *Race Ethnicity and Education, 8*(1), 69–91. https://doi.org/10.1080/1361332052000341006

4

Money Management

Understanding Personal Finances

John R. Jones III

As a midcareer professional, you have graduated from college, achieved some successes in launching a career, and obtained some basic understanding of financial literacy. You should have acquired a minimum knowledge of financial fundamentals such as budgeting, credit scores, interest rates, or borrowing money. But beyond those fundamentals, you should be determining both the depth of your financial literacy and whether it is preparing you for security (i.e., having enough money saved for emergency and future goals) in retirement.

Many first-generation college students come from families with limited means, which affects financial literacy. Without an understanding of rudimentary financial concepts, many parents of first-generation students were not well equipped to make prudent fiscal decisions. They could not educate their kids about such basic information as interest compounding and credit. Additionally, first-generation students had to both navigate the university landscape with zero or limited financial knowledge and, after graduation, learn how to apply their education to create professional and personal economic opportunities for themselves and, sometimes, their parents.

Not only does financial literacy explain financial behavior (Lusardi & de Bassa Scheresberg, 2013), but people with strong financial skills tend to do a better job at achieving financial security (Lusardi & Mitchell, 2014). As you assess your current state of financial literacy, you should note the following: (1) how your knowledge of dealing with debt influences how you manage your assets and liabilities; and (2) the effects of this knowledge on your retirement savings (Lusardi & de Bassa Scheresberg, 2013). Thus, the goal of this chapter is threefold: (1) to increase the reader's understanding of the effect of financial literacy; (2) to help the reader better understand debt; and (3) to improve the reader's financial knowledge in order to secure a better retirement.

This chapter will explain why deficiencies in financial literacy have existed among first-generation college graduates, while defining financial literacy and examining it in depth. Each subsequent section includes **do's** and **don'ts**. The section on debt reviews the pitfalls of amassing too many expenses—and encourages the reader to avoid it. Finally, the chapter emphasizes the financial elements necessary to navigate retirement planning and build a secure financial future.

Intergenerational Learning

In both traditional and modern cultures, intergenerational learning has been the informal vehicle within families for "systematic transfer of knowledge, skills, competencies, norms, and values between generations—and is as old as mankind" (Hoff, 2007, p. 126). Typically, the elders or grandparents of the family share wisdom and are esteemed for their role in perpetuating the values, culture, and uniqueness of the family. Parents also play a pivotal role in modeling behaviors and giving information to their children. Direct knowledge transfer from parents to children is often based on the wisdom or past experiences of the parents; therefore, today many first-generation students are underinformed because their parents were not college educated. They were not equipped to assist their children with such matters as financial literacy.

Many first-generation students come from families with depressed socioeconomic status, and the parents had very little formal education, including instruction in financial subjects. Indeed, research confirms that mothers' and fathers' education levels are positively correlated with financial literacy (Klapper et al., 2014). Women, the poor, and the less educated are more likely to suffer from gaps in financial knowledge (Klapper et al., 2014). In short, the way that parents manage (or not) their own finances has a considerable influence on how children learn financial literacy (Huddleston, 2020). If the parents lacked financial acumen, then so too will many first-generation students.

What is Financial Literacy?

The term *financial literacy* is defined as the combination of knowledge about finances with attitudes, skills, and behaviors that are important for making decisions based on personal circumstances (Complete Controller, 2018). A more comprehensive understanding of the term is best garnered from the work of Lusardi and Mitchell (2014). The authors identified three concepts that together shed light on people's financial decision making. This universal tool applies to every context and economic environment; it assesses not only what people know but also what they need to know—and then it evaluates the gap between the two. These three concepts are (1) the capacity to calculate interest rates and understand compound interest; (2) an understanding of inflation; and (3) the ability to comprehend risk diversification. The following questions elucidate Lusardi and Mitchell's (2014) research and its implications.

- Suppose you had $100 in a savings account and the interest rate was 2% per year. After 5 years, how much do you think you would have in the account if you left the money to grow? [more than $102; exactly $102; less than $102; do not know; refuse to answer]
  The answer is more than $102.

- Imagine that the interest rate on your savings account was 1% per year and inflation was 2% per year. After 1 year, would you be able to buy [more than today; exactly the same as; or less than today; do not know; refuse to answer] with the money in this account?
  The answer is less than today.

- Do you think that the following statement is true or false? "Buying a single company stock usually provides a safer return than a stock mutual fund." [true; false; do not know; refuse to answer].
  The answer is false.

The first question measures *numeracy,* or the capacity to do a simple calculation related to the compounding of interest rates. The second question measures understanding *inflation,* again in the context of a simple financial decision. The third question is a joint test of knowledge about stocks and stock mutual funds and of *risk diversification,* since the answer to this question depends on knowing what a stock is and that a mutual fund is composed of many stocks. As is clear from the theoretical models described earlier, many decisions about retirement savings must deal with financial markets. Accordingly, it is important to understand knowledge of the stock market, as well as differentiate between levels of financial knowledge.

(Lusardi & Mitchell, 2014, p. 10)

Compared with people of other nations, Americans fall short when it comes to financial literacy. Although the United States is the world's largest economy, the Standard & Poor's Global Financial Literacy Survey ranks it no. 14 in financial literacy (Klapper et al., 2014). In a separate study, only 30% of Americans were able to successfully answer the preceding financial questions about inflation, interest compounding, and risk diversification. One of the many unfortunate consequences to this financial illiteracy is that those individuals with lower financial literacy tend to buy on credit and are unable to pay their full balance each month—and end up spending more in interest (Zucchi, 2019).

In general, financial literacy is using your knowledge to make wise financial decisions that will benefit you throughout your life. More important, it provides you with the fundamentals to understand major money concepts such as debts, savings, investments, and emergencies. If you correctly answered the three questions above, you have basic financial literacy.

As previously noted, the financial education of first-generation students often does not happen during the intergenerational transfer of knowledge from their parents. Further, although 21 states require high school students to take a course in financial education (Council for Economic Education, 2020), many first-generation students did not benefit from this instruction because their schools lacked the resources to include it in the curriculum. On a positive note, although very few colleges or universities require a financial literacy course, most first-generation students see a sharp increase in their financial literacy with educational attainment (Klapper et al., 2014). In other words, as more first-generation students graduate from college, their financial literacy indirectly improves. With their career progression, they obtain more accounts (checking, savings, certificates of deposit, stocks, etc.) at financial institutions, resulting in increased financial literacy. Financial literacy may also grow during your career, particularly if you are tasked with managing a budget as part of your job. Financial knowledge obtained on the job, understandably, is transferable and will assist you in making better personal financial decisions.

In summary, financial education prepares consumers for big decisions and minimizes early mistakes (Iacurci, 2019). Financial education not only assists you in effectively handling your finances but also establishes a foundation to plan for retirement and mitigate later financial burdens (being a care giver, facing health issues). Part of your financial education occurs when you open an account at a financial institution; however, those account owners who lack financial knowledge may not be fully benefiting from what their banks have to offer (Klapper et al., 2014). It is tremendously important and beneficial to understand all accounts you own, especially because you will make many financial decisions: leasing versus buying a car, renting versus owning a home, taking out a fixed-rate mortgage versus one with an adjustable rate, and choosing the best type of life and health insurance to purchase (Iacurci, 2019). The next pages contain financial concepts (budgeting, debt, work benefits, retirement, emergency preparedness, etc.) that not only assist you in improving your literacy but are instrumental in achieving security at retirement.

Do's & Don'ts

Do

- Continue to become more financially literate—especially given that you may be managing your own retirement account, personal assets, and debt.
- Make sure to know all the benefits and risks when opening accounts at banks or financial institutions.

Don't

- Have a passive understanding of basic financial concepts. Learn how to actively save for retirement—especially since employees must save most of their money on their own in a 401(k) or individual retirement account (IRA). Decide how much you want to save and how to invest it.

- Buy on credit, especially if you don't fully understand the cost of interest.

Financially Inexperienced

There is a tremendous cost to being financially inexperienced. Individuals with lower levels of financial literacy exhibit uninformed borrowing behavior and debt management; they tend to accrue larger expenses and incur higher loan interest rates (Lusardi & de Bassa Scheresberg, 2013). The financially illiterate also report excessive debt loads and that they were unable to judge the impact of their inability to manage debt (Lusardi & de Bassa Scheresberg, 2013). Those individuals who are financially literate make more informed choices, particularly in saving, investing, and preparing for retirement. If you are financially inexperienced, you should work to overcome your knowledge deficit and avoid taking on debt.

Debt

Debt includes student loans, credit cards, auto loans, mortgages, home equity lines of credit, and other household debt. Household debt is defined as the combined expenses of all people in a household. A study commissioned by NerdWallet and conducted by The Harris Poll noted that in December 2019, the total owed by an average U.S. household was $7,104 in credit card debt, $192,618 in mortgage debt, $27,934 in auto loan debt, and $46,679 in student loan debt (el Issa, 2019). In another study, 60% of employees indicated that their level of debt was a problem, and 70% noted that their nonmortgage debt affected their ability to save for retirement (Employee Benefit Research Institute [EBRI] & Greenwald and Associates, 2019).

Credit card balances carried from one month to the next hit $466.2 billion in December 2019 (el Issa, 2019). This debt is one of the costliest: As of August 2019, the average annual percentage rate, or APR (*annual percentage rate* represents the actual yearly cost of funds over the term of a loan, credit card, etc.), on these accounts accrued 16.97% interest, according to the Federal Reserve Bank of St. Louis (el Issa, 2019). Credit card debt has increased more than 7% in the past year and almost 37% in the past 5 years (el Issa, 2019). U.S. households carrying credit card debt from month to month will pay more than $1,100 in interest in a year (el Issa, 2019). Eliminating this debt and then saving for retirement are the most important steps in achieving financial security.

Student loans are almost as commonplace as car loans; however, if you decide to go back to school for an advanced degree, make every effort to attend and graduate with no additional student loan debt. This means that instead of applying for a student loan, research and apply for one of the numerous scholarships that may be available. Another alternative to a student loan is identifying ways to earn additional income by working a second job or working overtime. If you do choose to go the student loan route, borrow as little as possible. A good rule of thumb: Never take on more in loans than you expect to earn in your first year after graduation (Farrington, 2019). Most borrowers get into trouble when their earning potential is substantially less than the loan amount; this often leads to the inability to pay off the loan. Also, underemployed individuals have greater difficulty meeting their financial obligations and undoubtedly prioritize necessities such as rent, food, and utilities above their student loan payments (Mitchell-Barney, 2018). Outstanding student loan debt in the United

States grew to more than \$1.5 trillion owed by almost 45 million Americans (Farrington, 2019). The average undergraduate borrower in the graduating class of 2019 had an average student loan debt of \$29,900 (Farrington, 2019).

Auto loan debt among Americans totals \$1.2 trillion and makes up 9.5% of all outstanding household debt (Fontinelle, 2020). Auto loans are the third-largest category of American household debt after mortgages (\$8.9 trillion) and student loans (\$1.5 trillion); debt in all three categories has increased steadily since 2011. When consumers assume more debt, they jeopardize their ability to have a financially secure retirement. Consumer debt is a concern today because it has reached record levels, and its rise comes as powerful trends—such as stagnating incomes, new forms of credit availability, and structural changes in medical and education markets—shape how debt is incurred and how it affects financial security (EPIC, 2018). This increasing debt could indicate that families are under financial stress and need to borrow to pay for necessities.

Do's & Don'ts

Do

- Eliminate all consumer debt as quickly as possible. Consider using the debt snowball method: List debts from smallest to largest, and as you pay off the smallest debt, roll what you used to pay toward it onto the next largest debt.

Don't

- Buy on credit. If you are unable to pay the balance in full, you end up spending more in interest.

Financial Skills

Budgeting

Several negative consequences can result from operating without a budget. Some common examples include a lack of or insufficient savings, less financial control of spending, a higher likelihood of going into debt, and greater financial stress (Buchenau, 2018). The longer you take to implement a budget, the more painful these consequences can become and the more difficult it will be to navigate unexpected expenses and achieve your financial goals (Buchenau, 2018). According to Buchenau (2018), not having a budget can result in the following:

- **Lack of savings:** When you don't know your exact monthly income or your total monthly expenses, it's much more difficult to save money. What you are able to save each month depends on how much you spend. A budget makes these amounts clear.

- **Less financial control:** Budgeting creates boundaries within your financial life. When you budget properly, it's easy to know how much money you can realistically spend on food, housing, automotive expenses, etc., while still staying on track to meet your financial goals.

- **Higher likelihood of more debt:** When you don't live on a budget, you lose the constant reminder of how harmful debt is on your financial life—which makes you more likely to go into more debt. And the more debt you take on, the more you reduce your net worth.

- **More financial stress:** One of the hardest financial obstacles to overcome is unforeseen expenses. When you're unprepared for the unexpected, you feel like you've lost financial control, you spend beyond your means, you're buried in debt, and you're unfulfilled by not achieving your financial goals.

A foundation of any successful financial plan involves a detailed, up-to-date budget that shows what money is coming into your account each month and what expenses are going out (Hoyt, 2019). More specifically, a budget maps out your expected income; fixed expenses (housing cost, utilities, food, insurance, transportation costs, etc.); discretionary expenses (vacations, entertainment, dining out, hobbies, etc.); emergency reserve; retirement; and kids' college savings. First and foremost, your monthly income should be more than your monthly expenses. Next, subtract all expenses from your income. Then take the balance and apply it to your goals (e.g., a special vacation, new car, house, retirement, furthering your education). If your monthly expenses are more than your monthly income, then you'll need to revise your spending habits so you can live within your means (Hoyt, 2019). Also, if at the end of the month, your monthly income barely covers your monthly fixed expenses without even contributing to savings, an emergency fund, or your retirement, then you need to identify ways to decrease your fixed expenses and/or increase your income. Some ways to reduce your fixed expenses include cutting back on the number of times that you eat out or visit your coffee shop or assessing whether your vehicle purchase was the "right size" for your budget (the rule of thumb is to spend no more than 20% of your take-home pay on your car). If you cannot reduce your fixed expenses, then you will need to boost your income to avoid running up debt.

A solid budget provides a path toward achieving your financial goals and gives you a way to guard against any financial fallout from unforeseen expenses. If you are already using a budget to help manage your finances, ensure that you are assessing its effectiveness annually, because your income and expenses will change. Note that creating a budget is not a complicated process; it can be as easy as using the 50/20/30 rule (Forbes, 2016):

- 50% of your income should go to living expenses and essentials; this includes your rent, utilities, and things like groceries and transportation for work.
- 20% of your income should go to financial goals; this means your savings, investments, and debt-reduction payments.
- 30% of your income should be used for flexible spending; this is everything you buy that you want but don't necessarily need (like money spent on entertainment and travel).

A successful budget will help you do the following:

1. Follow a monthly spending plan. This will allow you to identify where you are spending your money each month and to prioritize your household needs.
2. Identify ways to lower your monthly bills and clearly show where you are spending your money, so that you are motivated to eliminate extraneous or discretionary expenses (e.g., entertainment, dining out, daily coffee outings, hobbies, etc.).
3. Pay off accrued debt.
4. Distinguish between short-, medium-, and long-term goals. (Ask yourself: What are your financial goals? Plan a dream vacation? Further your education? Buy a new car or house? Retire early? Write down the goals that are most important and identify a timeline to help you get there.)

Do's & Don'ts

Do

- Review your expenses and spending habits to maximize your savings for goals.
- Revisit your financial goals frequently to stay motivated in achieving them.

- Establish an emergency fund to cover unexpected events (e.g., furlough or loss of job, weather emergency, illness).

Don't
- Forget to anticipate costs that aren't monthly (e.g., holiday spending, home maintenance, donations to charity).
- Let discretionary expenses (e.g., vacations, entertainment, dining out, hobbies, etc.) take precedence over saving for retirement.
- Just have a plan, actively and faithfully follow your plan.

Employee Benefits

Are you using your employee benefits to the fullest potential? According to a study by the American Institute of Certified Professional Accountants (AICPA; 2018a), even though employed Americans place a great value on the benefits offered to them by their employers, only 3 out of 10 employees are very confident that they are utilizing them to their fullest potential. AICPA noted that although nearly 9 in 10 employed adults (88%) felt confident that they understood all the benefits available to them when they accepted their current job, only 28% feel very confident that they are using their benefits to their fullest potential. Greg Anton, chairman of AICPA's National CPA Financial Literacy Commission, noted, "Leaving benefits underutilized should be treated the same way if workers were not 100 percent confident in receiving all the money in their paycheck. Americans need to take time to truly understand their benefits and make sure they're not leaving any money on the table" (AICPA, 2018a, para. 6).

Do's & Don'ts

Do

- Take the time to understand your workplace benefits; perhaps meet with someone in human resources.
- Use your benefits to the fullest and incorporate them into your financial planning.

Don't

- Make the same benefit elections automatically when your open enrollment information arrives. Answer the following questions to ensure that you are making the best choices (AICPA, 2018c):

  - Are there any changes to my personal situation that might make another health insurance choice more valuable?
  - What did I pay for out of pocket this year that could be covered by an insurance option next year (e.g., dental or vision insurance)? Could I pay with pretax dollars through an FSA [flexible savings account] or HSA [health savings account]?
  - What changes can I make to my budget to allow me to increase my tax deferral savings through my FSA or HSA?

Financial Emergencies Fund

Unexpected life events happen, and they usually bring with them some substantial costs. An estimated 40% of Americans cannot afford a $400 emergency expense (Board of Governors of the Federal Reserve System, 2019). To lessen the financial impact of an unexpected event, you should be intentional about establishing an emergency fund to cover 3 to 6 months of expenses. The COVID-19 pandemic of 2020 demonstrates why it is important to have an emergency fund. During this time, many employees experienced a disruption in work that resulted in a reduced or no paycheck.

An emergency fund is money you set aside in a savings or money market account that is reserved exclusively for unexpected events that will require more cash than you usually have on hand (AICPA, 2018b). This special emergency fund will allow you to cover the expenses without having to pull from other designated savings/retirement funds or go further in debt by charging credit cards. The amount that you set aside in your emergency fund depends on your debt and current financial needs. Before you establish your emergency fund, you should first eliminate all consumer debt.

Do's & Don'ts

Do
- Set aside enough money to cover 3 to 6 months of expenses.
- Keep your emergency fund in something that is liquid, like a money market or savings account.

Don't
- Establish this fund until all consumer debt is eliminated.

- Establish a pattern of living above your means and spending more than you earn.

Retirement

For many employees, pensions have all but disappeared. So, one of the biggest financial decisions an employee must make is how to save for retirement, which could mean (1) saving the majority of your money on your own in a 401(k) plan or IRA; (2) deciding how much you need to save; and (3) deciding how to invest that money (Iacurci, 2019). Unfortunately, many employees are not doing a good job of saving or preparing for retirement. Nearly half of Americans don't expect to have enough money to retire comfortably (Nova, 2018) and less than two fifths of them believe that they are on track with their savings (Board of Governors of the Federal Reserve System, 2019). From another study, nearly 90% of retirees rely on Social Security as a source of income in retirement (EBRI & Greenwald and Associates, 2019).

Early-Career Planning

The best time to start planning and saving for retirement is early in your career. The earlier you start saving for retirement, the more time your money has to accumulate interest. The following quote shows you the benefit of time in adding *accumulated interest* back to the principal sum, so that interest is earned on top of interest from that moment on.

For example, say you're 30 years old with nothing saved for retirement, and you can only manage to save $100 per month. If you're earning a 7 percent annual rate of return on your investments, you'd have around $166,000 saved by age 65. In another scenario, say you held off on saving anything until age 45, but you started saving $300 per month. If you're still earning a 7 percent return, you'd have around $147,000 saved by age 65. So even though you'd be saving three times as much, it doesn't make up for getting off to a late start. (Brockman, 2019, p. 1)

Although employees are more confident that they know how much money they need to live comfortably in retirement, just 40% have tried to calculate that amount (EBRI & Greenwald and Associates, 2019). Early in your career is a good time to establish a pattern of living within your means and avoiding the temptation to buy more as you earn more (Silvestrini, 2019).

It is beneficial not only to determine how much you need for retirement but also to start saving whatever you can early in your career and increase your contributions as you earn more. If your employer has a retirement savings plan, you should participate, especially if it offers matching funds. At a minimum, by participating in your employer's retirement savings plan, you will receive a tax benefit from saving pretax funds (Silvestrini, 2019). In other words, by contributing to a pre-tax investment account first, you are saving money that you don't have to pay income tax on until you withdraw it. If you don't have access to a 401(k), then your next best option is an IRA. These tax-advantaged retirement accounts come with the same major tax benefits as a 401(k), though they will not have an employer match. To establish a robust retirement plan that will sustain you during your "golden years," you should consider these questions (Silvestrini, 2019):

- At what age do you hope to retire?
- What do you plan to do in retirement?
- How many years do you think you'll live after you retire?
- What are your sources of income during retirement?

- How long do you have to save?
- How are you going to account for risks, including inflation?

The planning strategies you implement depend on your career stage, financial goals, the age at which you would like to retire, and your current financial situation (Silvestrini, 2019). If you are early in your professional career, have little or no debt, and have started saving for retirement, the factor of having more time to invest and more interest compounding will benefit you more than if you were late in your career and had a shorter amount of time to invest. Given that your planning strategies depend on the aforementioned variables, you should consult with a certified financial planner to achieve the greatest amount of retirement savings.

As you enter midcareer (40s and 50s), continue to focus on eliminating debt and building on your retirement plan. If you have not already eliminated all consumer debt, your top priority should be to do so. Next, if you haven't started saving or aren't making maximum contributions to your savings, start as soon as possible. If all consumer debt is eliminated and the only payment you have is a mortgage or rent, you should invest at least 15% of your before-tax gross income in order to have a financially secure retirement (Ramsey, 2013). This time of your career tends to be your peak earning years, so be laser focused in your efforts to boost your earnings and your savings for retirement (Silvestrini, 2019).

For a successful retirement plan, answer the following questions:

1. Have you identified your retirement age? In order to appropriately save the targeted dollar amount that would sustain you, you must identify your retirement age and anticipated life expectancy. If you plan to retire before age 65, be sure to include the cost of health insurance, because you are not eligible for Medicare until after that age.

2. Will you have additional income or expenses during retirement? The response to this question will also help you to determine the targeted dollar amount needed for retirement.

3. How long do you have to save, and what is the targeted dollar amount?

4. What are some anticipated risks? What additional savings are needed to address medical costs, dental expenses, long-term care costs, and family needs?

Do's & Don'ts

Do
- Start early in planning and saving for retirement—after paying off all consumer debt.
- Spend less than you earn; after paying off your debt, invest the difference.
- Participate in your employer's retirement savings match program.
- Check annually to see if your investments still align with your goals and risk tolerances.
- Contribute to an IRA and try to make the maximum contributions.
- Consult with a financial planner to make sure you are on track.

Don't
- Touch your retirement savings or borrow against it.
- Don't forgot about health costs during retirement—Medicare does not cover all health care expenses in retirement.

Conclusion

If you could envision financial security during retirement, what does it look like and how will you make it a reality? Certainly, it will not occur by happenstance. In addition to having goals and a plan, you must *actively* follow your plan to make your vision come true. Reaching financial security during retirement may involve accessing and overcoming a financial knowledge deficit, navigating around bad financial decisions, or increasing the amounts saved for retirement. Generally, the financial behavior/knowledge that has led you to this point in your career may not be the solution for financial security at retirement: What may have gotten you here, may not get you there. You may have to increase your financial knowledge or change your behavior, particularly if it is affecting your ability to reach financial security.

At this midpoint in life, everyone wants to take extravagant vacations, drive a new car, or overindulge on jewelry or fashion. Often the problem is that people engage in these expenses when they cannot afford them. Do not go into debt or make your debt larger by succumbing to buying those things in the moment when you do not have money in the bank. Your goal should be to focus on reaching financial security before and after retirement—without taking on debt.

Take time not only to understand what is being said in this chapter but also to fully engage and make it part of your financial literacy. At the end of the day—and perhaps the end of your successful professional career—you will reach retirement. When making current financial decisions, you should keep financial security at retirement at top of mind.

Questions for Reflection

1. What were the main messages you received from your parents/guardians regarding finances? How have those messages been helpful in your life (personal and professional)?

2. If you have kids, how are you helping them to become financially literate? What financial mistakes did you make, and how are you using what you learned to instruct your kids?

3. What item(s) did you purchase that contributed to creating significant debt? If you could hit replay, would you make the same decision(s)? How did that decision affect your financial goals?

4. What are your best financial strategies at work? How do these strategies translate into making better personal financial decisions?

5. What is your retirement plan? How are you planning financially for your retirement? Are you on track to meet your financial goals? If not, what adjustment are you making?

References

American Institute of Certified Professional Accountants. (2018a). *AICPA survey.* https://www.aicpa.org/press/pressreleases/2018/americans-favor-workplace-benefits-over-extra-salary.html

American Institute of Certified Professional Accountants. (2018b). *Being financially prepared in an emergency!* https://www.360financialliteracy.org/Topics/In-Crisis/Preparedness/Be-Financially-Prepared-in-an-Emergency%21

American Institute of Certified Professional Accountants. (2018c). *5 questions to ask yourself this open enrollment season from the AICPA.* https://www.360financialliteracy.org/About-360/For-the-Press/5-Questions-to-Ask-Yourself-This-Open-Enrollment-Season-from-the-AICPA

Board of Governors of the Federal Reserve System. (2019, May). *Report on the economic well-being of U.S. households in 2018.* https://www.federalreserve.gov/publications/2019-economic-well-being-of-us-households-in-2018-economic-well-being.htm

Brockman, K. (2019, April 10). Only 1 in 10 Americans are financially prepared: How do you stack up? *The Motley Fool.* https://www.fool.com/retirement/2019/04/10/only-1-in-10-americans-are-financially-prepared-ho.aspx

Buchenau, Z. (2018). 8 painful consequences of not budgeting. *Be the Budget.* https://bethebudget.com/consequences-of-not-budgeting

Complete Controller. (2018, June). *3 serious problems with the concept of 'financial literacy.'* https://www.completecontroller.com/3-serious-problems-with-the-concept-of-financial-literacy

Council for Economic Education. (2020). *Economic and personal finance education in our nation's schools—Survey of the states.* https://www.councilforeconed.org/wp-content/uploads/2020/02/2020-Survey-of-the-States.pdf

el Issa, E. (2019, December 2). 2019 American household credit card debt study. *NerdWallet.* https://www.nerdwallet.com/blog/household-credit-card-debt-study-2019

Employee Benefit Research Institute, & Greenwald and Associates. (2019, April 23). *2019 retirement confidence survey summary report.* https://www.ebri.org/docs/default-source/rcs/2020-rcs/2020-rcs-summary-report.pdf?sfvrsn=84bc3d2f_7

EPIC (The Aspen Institute's Expanding Prosperity Impact Collaborative). (2018). *Lifting the weight: Solving the consumer debt crisis for families, communities, & future generations.* http://www.aspenepic.org/wp-content/uploads/2018/12/LiftingtheWeight_SolutionsFramework.pdf

Farrington, R. (2019, December 30). Average student loan debt by year (graduating class). *The College Investor.* https://thecollegeinvestor.com/32031/average-student-loan-debt-by-year

Fontinelle, A. (2020, January 13). American debt: Auto loan balances total $1.2 trillion in 2020. *Investopedia.* https://www.investopedia.com/personal-finance/american-debt-auto-loan-debt

Forbes. (2016, July 11). New to budgeting? Why you should try the 50-20-30 rule. *Forbes.* https://www.forbes.com/sites/trulia/2016/07/11/new-to-budgeting-why-you-should-try-the-50-20-30-rule/#b0b82332e94e

Hoff, A. (2007). Intergenerational learning as an adaptation strategy in aging knowledge societies. In European Commission (Ed.), *Education, employment, Europe* (pp. 126–129). National Contact Point for Research Programmes of the European Union.

Hoyt, E. (2019, August 20). The 5 key components of financial literacy. *Fast Web.* https://www.fastweb.com/student-life/articles/the-5-key-components-of-financial-literacy

Huddleston, C. (2020, February). How to teach your kids good money habits. *Forbes.* https://www.forbes.com/advisor/personal-finance/how-to-teach-your-kids-good-money-habits

Iacurci, G. (2019). Financial literacy: An epic fail in America. *Investment News.* https://www.investmentnews.com/financial-literacy-an-epic-fail-in-america-78385

Klapper, L., Lusardi, A., & Van Oudheusden, P. (2014). *Financial literacy around the world: Insights from the Standard & Poor's Ratings Services Global Financial Literacy Survey.* https://responsiblefinanceforum.org/wp-content/uploads/2015/12/2015-Finlit_paper_17_F3_SINGLES.pdf

Lusardi, A., & de Bassa Scheresberg, C. (2013). *Financial literacy and high-cost borrowing in the United States* (NBER Working Paper 18969). National Bureau of Economic Research. https://doi.org/10.3386/w18969

Lusardi, A., & Mitchell, O. S. (2014, March). The economic importance of financial literary: Theory and evidence. *Journal of Economic Literature, 52*(1), 5–44. https://doi.org/10.1257/jel.52.1.5

Mitchell-Barney, J. (2018, February 19). 5 factors that contribute to student loan delinquency. *The Windham Professionals.* https://www.windhampros.com/student-loan-delinquency-factors

Nova, A. (2018, May 9). Almost half of Americans don't expect to have enough money to retire comfortably—but there's some good news. *Investor Toolkit.* https://www.cnbc.com/2018/05/09/almost-half-of-americans-dont-expect-to-have-enough-money-to-retire-comfortably—but-theres-some-good-news.html

Ramsey, D. (2013). *The total money makeover: A proven plan for financial fitness.* Nelson Press.

Silvestrini, E. (2019). Retirement planning. *Annuity.* https://www.annuity.org/retirement/planning

Zucchi, K. (2019). *Why financial literacy is so important.* Dechtman Wealth Management. https://dechtmanwealth.com/why-financial-literacy-is-so-important

PART II

Purposeful Interaction

5

Resilience

First-generation Professionals Persist

La'Tonya Rease Miles and Danette D. Buie

First-generation students are often described as possessing or in need of resilience or grit (Alcock & Belluigi 2018; Azmitia et al., 2018; Clauss-Ehlers & Wibrowski, 2007; Reed et al., 2019). It is often presumed that a first-generation student—by virtue of being admitted to college—is persistent and has overcome many barriers. The research on resilience and first-generation college students predominantly is situated in the undergraduate student experience. While there is emerging research on the resilience of first-generation student affairs practitioners, there is considerably less dialogue about their experience at the mid-level.

In this chapter, we posit a resilience model for first-generation professionals, drawing on contemporary popular psychology literature and our own professional experiences as Black first-generation college graduates from working-class backgrounds. We discuss the hidden curriculum, or unwritten rules and expectations, of the student affairs workplace, and we offer several tips to help first-generation mid-level professionals prosper during adverse times. We also address our sometimes-fraught relationship with the field, including our frustration with the proverbial glass ceiling that thwarts our own progress as women leaders.

Before we consider first-generation professionals and resilience, it is important to explore the college experience and the importance of resilience relative to the identity of a first-generation college student. Resilience typically is defined as the ability to thrive in the face of adversity (Gordon, 1996). It can be described further as a characteristic based on experiences, personal growth, and development in overcoming barriers and unfavorable conditions (Connor & Davidson, 2003). Environment and personal factors can also increase an individual's competence and shape resilience (Gordon, 1996). Both of us identify as Black cis-women from working-class backgrounds, and we were raised by single Black women who became pregnant as teenagers. By all indicators, we were incredibly unlikely to go to college, much less graduate and go on to earn doctorates.[1] Clearly, we cultivated considerable resilience to achieve these goals, but we also acknowledge the various support systems and mentors who encouraged us along the way.

Resilience tends to be comingled with first-generation identity because the label "first-generation" is often associated with negative stereotypes concerning struggle and hardship. These stereotypes can affect students' identity and self-esteem, as first-generation college students may arrive to campus with doubts about their ability to achieve; these students then may develop an internal deficit identity that impacts their social and academic experiences in college (Alessandria & Nelson, 2005; Orbe, 2008). Deficit-based research or narratives focus more on perceived gaps and weaknesses; strengths-based research or narratives highlight talents and assets (Lopez & Louis, 2009).

---

[1] In 2002, 37% of doctorate recipients reported that neither parent had completed a college degree (Hoffer, 2003).

Between resilience and first-generation college students lies an interdependent relationship: The identification of resilience depends on the identification of adversity (Rutter, 2007). In other words, adversity must be present for resilience to exist, and the literature indicates an endless disparity in educational outcomes between first-generation students and their non-first-generation peers. In terms of these two groups, research has shown that first-generation students are less likely to persist and graduate from college (Pike & Kuh, 2005; Warburton et al., 2001). According to Franke et al. (2011), a 14.7% gap exists between first-generation and non-first-generation students (24.7% and 42.1%, respectively) at the 4-year degree attainment rate, and the 6-year gap remained the same for both groups, at 14%. According to Stephens et al. (2012), the gap in educational outcomes between first-generation students and continuing-generation students stems from differences in the groups' social and economic status, which can affect levels of social and cultural capital (Soria & Stebleton, 2012) and ultimately shape engagement and intellectual development in college (Pike & Kuh, 2005).[2]

Much scholarly and popular literature frame the first-generation college experience in deficit language, using such terms as *disadvantaged, low-achieving, vulnerable*, and *at-risk* to describe first-generation students (Wildhagen, 2015). La'Tonya recalls learning that her background is "working-class" while taking a sociology course one summer at a local college, and it was not until graduate school that she realized a summer camp she attended in junior high was for "at-risk" youth; all she knew was that it was free. These labels contribute to a dominant narrative that promotes misunderstanding and limits the capacity of practitioners, researchers, and policymakers to effectively grasp how the backgrounds and identities of students shape their decisions and relationships to others. Moreover, such categorizations overlook the strengths and funds

---

[2] Resilience needs to be problematized, too, because it often focuses on what students needs to experience in order to be successful rather than on how institutions need to change.

of knowledge that minoritized and historically underrepresented students already possess (Vélez-Ibáñez & Greenberg, 1992). Thankfully, more recent literature about first-generation college students takes a more asset-based approach, recognizing, for instance, that resilience itself is a form of capital.

Many researchers and practitioners, for example, have offered counter-narratives of the first-generation identity, with a focus on empowerment, community, and resilience (Anderson, 2006; Coles, 2012; Horn & Chen, 1998; Moschetti & Hudley, 2015; Orbe, 2008). The cultivation of a resilient mindset by first-generation students positively influences postsecondary success because it helps them to see their potential and recognize they are capable of achievement (Orbe, 2008). To be the first to do anything takes courage, but it also takes buoyancy and flexibility. It is important to recognize that individuals from underrepresented backgrounds (e.g., low-income, first-generation, minority) can and do thrive despite adversity and unfavorable conditions.

This recognition constitutes a framework like that of "aspirational capital," which Yosso (2005) defined as "the ability to maintain hopes and dreams for the future, even in the face of real and perceived barriers" (p. 10). Yosso claimed that family members demonstrate this form of capital when they nurture dreams and hopes for their children and future generations, even when their current circumstances (e.g., financial resources, educational attainment) would act as a deterrent. Aspirational capital is future oriented and encourages a person to persist. For the purposes of this chapter, we wonder: What happens once those ambitious aspirations are realized—that is, when a parent's dreams are actualized and their child graduates college, obtains a graduate degree, and then becomes a mid-level professional? As we shall discuss later in this chapter, that child, who has surpassed their parents' own educational level and, most likely, their parents' professional status as well, must learn how to navigate new arenas and, we argue, must *internalize* aspirational capital and cultivate resilience in order to thrive in the professional workforce.

Moving From First-generation Student to First-generation Professional: The Hidden Curriculum in the Workplace

The theme of resilience holds true in contexts beyond those of higher education, especially for first-generation professionals. This cohort typically faces experiences similar to those encountered in college, such as thriving in the face of adversity, overcoming barriers and unfavorable conditions, and navigating both the hidden curriculum and workplace expectations. Generally, the term *hidden curriculum* refers to a set of tacit expectations and unspoken protocols that guide values and social behaviors in academe (Margolis, 2001). Usually not taught explicitly, these rules, behaviors, and expectations are unwritten and unofficial and may further marginalize already disadvantaged groups, such as first-generation college students, the poor and working classes, and people of color.

Unspoken protocols and social behaviors also exist in the workplace; every industry, including student affairs, has its own set of rules and expectations that must be learned. For example, relationship management is an important attribute to learn in the student affairs profession. It is essentially the ability to maintain strong relationships that drive solutions and outcomes (Bourdieu, 1986; Hirt et al., 2005). Reputation is a form of social capital for mid-level professionals; it marks their ability to become trusted strategic partners to senior leaders. Building these relationships requires that the professional understand institutional pain points, ask questions, and understand the motivations, constraints, strengths, and opportunities at hand. It is often implied and surely expected that midcareer professionals "manage up," or anticipate a supervisor's needs—especially if that supervisor is a senior leader on campus.

This element of the hidden curriculum may continue to thwart first-generation professionals, given that their work environments typically differ greatly from those of their parents or guardians (Gibbons, 2014; Olson, 2014; Storlie et al., 2016; Tate et al., 2015). As a result, first-generation professionals are often left to figure things out on their own—even well into their careers. Danette's mother, for instance, tried her best to help Danette navigate entering the workforce, but the two women's career pathways and professional experiences were too dissimilar. Danette's mom has not completed high school, and Danette had to build a new skill set as she navigated the unwritten rules of the workplace in the public and private sector. As she continued to progress in her career as a student affairs professional, Danette realized that certain unwritten rules spanned roles and institutions. For example, to achieve developmental goals and student learning outcomes, a student affairs professional must understand the unique characteristics of academic affairs and be able to navigate shared governance with faculty. Most of Danette's experience in academic affairs centered on creating a holistic student development approach by building relationships with faculty to advance student learning in cocurricular activities. The nature of fostering relationships holds true even in other industries, where collaborating with cross-functional partners is critical to success.

Danette attributes her career success to her ability to recognize the difference between being her authentic self and being the person others want her to be; advocating for herself; addressing conflict independently (through informal channels or formal reporting); getting coworkers to understand her value to the organization; engaging with cross-functional stakeholders to gain allies throughout the organization; and cultivating a community whose members can empathize with her experience (e.g., resource centers, employee resource groups). Chapter 2, on imposter syndrome, elaborates on these points.

Whereas new professionals may experience a grace period when it comes to learning the proverbial ropes, seasoned employees— particularly those who have obtained advanced or terminal degrees, who supervise full-time staff, or who are in leadership roles (i.e., mid-level professionals or higher)—are often expected to "hit the ground running." Author and leadership expert Jesse Sostrin (2016) elaborated on this discrepancy: "Nobody trained you to succeed in this hidden work, and you have to learn how to confront its every-day pitfalls. And although you can reach out to trusted colleagues for input, the pace of work and pressure to perform often limit our willingness to reflect, formulate questions, and take the time to seek guidance," (para. 4) particularly at the midcareer level, when it is assumed you know better. It is also worth noting that entry-level professionals in student affairs often have more structured onboard-ing experiences in the workplace; for example, they may be assigned a formal or informal mentor, may be hired in clusters or cohorts, and typically encouraged to ask questions and seek support.

Adversity in the Workplace

First-generation professionals often have experiences in the work-place that are similar to those of their first-generation counterparts in college. Adversity at work can sometimes lead to frustrations, stress, and anxiety about one's performance and career trajectory, and it may trigger imposter syndrome, as well. This section explores how these challenges may uniquely impact mid-level first-generation professionals and, in our case, women of color in particular.

The Accidental Administrator: La'Tonya's Story

Student affairs professionals often are viewed as role models of resil-ience as they help students navigate changes or difficult experiences.

In many cases, students, especially first-generation students, are introduced to the profession via residence hall directors, advisors, and the like (i.e., professionals who may have mentored them during college). Once inspired to join the field—often with the desire to pay it forward—an aspiring student affairs professional must then learn how to be an entry-level practitioner and, later, a midcareer professional. It is noteworthy that the pathways to success in higher education are less visible and less prescriptive than in other fields, making progress elusive.

I entered student affairs on accident as a mid-level professional. In fact, as I was completing my PhD in English, I had every intention of becoming a tenure-track faculty member. A colleague suggested that I apply to be a faculty in residence at the university, which would expose me for the first time to the office of residential life and, eventually, the division of student affairs. It was through this program that I learned about career options in this newly discovered field—even though I was several years into my work as an adjunct professor and full-time academic administrator. I learned quickly that academic affairs operates differently than student affairs, where faculty often are regarded with mild trepidation and suspicion—if they are thought of at all for student support services. In academic affairs, there definitely was less hugging and even fewer ice breakers. My previous faculty training plus my first-generation college background meant that I had to figure out how to navigate the institutional politics of student affairs with little guidance and no mentor.

One of the biggest challenges I faced while learning to be a mid-level student affairs professional who also identifies as Black, female, and working class was managing stress and workplace conflict, especially when seeking to advance within the workplace. Like many working-class individuals, I was raised in a family where I would get into trouble for not fighting back or speaking up for myself, and I was expected to handle confrontation directly, including in the workplace. My mother, who spent 5 years in the army, worked her way up from being an administrative assistant to the office manager and right hand to the CEO of a nonprofit. Until retirement, my grandmother was a homemaker who was paid "under the table" to babysit for other Black families. They passed down considerable confidence and were tremendous role models of determination and persistence, and they stressed the importance of women, Black women especially, speaking up. But how do those particular approaches translate to the field of higher education—specifically student affairs—when being direct is typically frowned upon? My mother's frank advice ("Give them a piece of your mind!") could only get me so far in this arena when seeking a raise or a promotion.

In the next section we discuss personal resilience as a strategy for surviving, thriving, and maintaining dignity in the face of workplace adversity.

A Resilience Model for First-generation Mid-Level Student Affairs Professionals

Although academic resilience is a commonly researched topic and shown to be necessary beyond academe, resilience in the workplace or employee resilience has yet to reach the same level of concern, despite many human resource professionals reporting higher rates of depression and anxiety, burnout, stress, and compassion fatigue among employees (Bardoel et al., 2014; Rees et al., 2015). Despite this gap in research, we posit a resilience model that is grounded in positive psychology and that embraces mindfulness, self-efficacy, and psychological adjustment (coping). According to Anderson et al. (2000), the primary reason for burnout among student affairs professionals is job stress from heavy workloads, perennial changes in the work environment, and decreased resources. More specifically, mid-level professionals identified unclear role expectations, limited career growth, and lack of recognition as primary job stressors (Johnsrud, 1996). Therefore, it is important to posit a resilience model grounded in positive psychology, as it is embedded in psychological capital, attitudes, and behavior. Yosso (2005) further reminded us that resilience itself is a form of capital.

Mindfulness

An important component to this framework, mindfulness is the ability to be fully present and to think about what is going on and what can be done about a stressful situation (Davis & Hayes, 2011). Several techniques allow you to practice mindfulness, including breathing exercises that focus on finding peace within yourself, writing your thoughts down or journaling, and spending less time worrying or over-analyzing the future. For example, one could establish short and long-term goals. The nature of the work and unrealistic expectations placed on student affairs professionals (sometimes requiring a 24/7 commitment) necessitates that they be more mindful of their obligations to themselves—for example, maintaining a work–life balance, keeping stress levels in check, and having a positive well-being (Guthrie et al., 2005). Student affairs practitioners often serve as first responders for students and tend to play a critical role in a campus crisis, so managing stress is important. For example, in the event of a student death, many details may require a professional's active attention, and they can be overwhelming to manage. These details include notifying the student's family, working with local and campus police officials, removing the student's belongings from campus, and coordinating mental health support services for students, faculty, and staff. Managing the full plate of the student affairs profession, which includes such unexpected crises, requires not only mindfulness but also a certain level of resilience. According to Burke et al. (2016), participating in mindfulness practices can positively affect the quality of service that student affairs professionals provide their students; it can also decrease workplace anxiety for these professionals and improve aspects of their personal, emotional, and physical well-being.

Self-efficacy

Self-efficacy, another component essential to this framework, is a cognitive process grounded in a person's belief in their ability to succeed in specific situations. Self-efficacy is intrinsically linked to psychological adjustment, based on the way a person manages stress or adversity (Maddux, 2013; Schwarzer & Warner, 2013). According to Benight and Cieslack (2011), using positive coping self-efficacy (confidence) to manage the demands of stress promotes positive self-cognition, increases motivation to achieve, and promotes effective decision making, in other words resilience.

Psychological Adjustment

Also part of this framework, psychological adjustment is the cognitive process induced from conflict between an internal thought and/or external obstacles in an attempt to restore one's sense of control and positive self-view (Helgeson et al., 2014; Taylor & Brown, 1988). Adjustment, also described as coping, is the ability to maintain high self-esteem, personal control, and an optimistic outlook in the face of challenges (Taylor & Brown, 1988; Terry et al., 1995). Sometimes this process can be described as the "fight or flight response" that our brain uses to process perceived threats. In student affairs we often work in high-stress environments that require us to adjust to ever-changing situations. According to Liu et al. (2014), self-esteem mediates the relationship between resilience and psychological adjustment because resilient individuals are often associated with positive characteristics that reflect an internal locus of control, optimism, and a positive self-view. The way we choose to cope in very stressful environments is important to our well-being and mental health as professionals, and it can affect our ability to thrive in the workplace.

Resilience is a process, but it plays a significant role in managing both adverse situations and positive stress. Like academic resilience, workplace resilience can be influenced by stress, environment, and personal characteristics; however, through practicing mindfulness, self-efficacy, and psychological adjustment, student affairs practitioners can promote positive adaptation while maintaining the energy and positive attitude needed for work in the profession. We view resilience as a positive personality trait that allows individuals to bounce back from adversity, adapt, and thrive in the face of difficulty. To give an example of this resilience model, Danette presents herself as a case study.

Down but Not Out: Danette's Story

In 2016 to 2017 the state of Illinois faced a budget impasse that affected funding across all institutions of higher education. At the time, I was working at a private 4-year school and realized my job might be affected as the institution's executive staff considered ways to reduce expenses. The university conducted several town hall meetings and discussed alternative options to prevent a reduction in force, including merging academic colleges, phasing out low-enrollment programs, and offering early-retirement incentives. I remember having a transparent conversation with my manager, an associate dean for the college. He urged me to seek new employment opportunities, as there was no guarantee that my job would not be eliminated. I embarked on a 4-month spree of job applications and interviews and sought out opportunities locally and in other states. At the time, I was only a program administrator; however, I was completing tasks that were considerably advanced.

So, I took a chance and started applying for director and assistant dean roles, and I was invited for an on-campus interview for an assistant dean position at the University of California, Santa Cruz. I received overwhelmingly positive feedback, but the hiring committee had another role for me in mind, one that better aligned with my background and research interests. This position had not been created, although the university had a student success and equity need for their academic division. Finally, after 25 job applications, 13 interviews, 3 job offers, and 1 week of salary negotiations, I officially accepted the inaugural role of director of student opportunity, success, and equity and left Chicago for California.

There were many obstacles in my journey to a mid-level professional; however, I used the resilience model we describe here. I believed in myself and my ability to confront challenges. I adapted, made meaning every day, and remained hopeful.

Conclusion

Resilience is a muscle that, with practice, can be strengthened as you grow and experience new things. *Resilience* is a buzzword in academia currently; however, many articles, podcasts, and online sources promote helpful strategies only *up to a point*. The key is to cultivate persistence and motivation beyond college graduation and landing your first job. First-generation professionals, especially those in mid-level positions, must not rely solely on self-determination in order to advance and succeed.

Questions for Reflection

Based on the resilience model and drawing upon our professional experiences, we recommend several tips and reflection questions to help first-generation professionals prosper during difficult times.

1. Not every situation is in your control and there may be external forces affecting your work environment, but positive psychological capital (which also can be described as growth mindset) is equally important in the workplace. In other words, to collectively turn challenges into opportunity, progress, and innovation, reframe your challenges and draw on your many strengths and prior experiences. As a first-generation professional, you have a unique opportunity to set new goals and strive for continuous improvement—not perfection. **What are your short and long-term professional goals?**

2. No one is ever too advanced to have a mentor or several mentors. You might consider these individuals as your own personal advisory board who can offer diplomatic advice. To fully make the most of the relationship and grow professionally, make sure these mentors have reached a senior level. **Have you identified anyone in your professional network as a mentor or sponsor, not just an advocate or ally?**

3. Continue to network both at your place of employment and in the community. Consider joining a student affairs support group/learning community or

lean into alumni Greek letter organizations, if applicable. **Are you involved in any of NASPA's learning communities or other professional associations?**

4. Take advantage of online communities, such as LinkedIn and Facebook groups—especially those that are relevant to your work. These spaces provide opportunities for you to stay current in the field and to expand your network—two things that can lead to greater work satisfaction and a renewed sense of purpose. **Have you refreshed your LinkedIn profile lately?**

5. On LinkedIn, add five higher education professionals whose careers align with your overall professional goals or trajectory. LinkedIn is a great place to share your accomplishments with peers, such as promotions, while also elevating your professional brand. This is especially useful if you are not currently receiving validation in your workspace. **Have you considered reaching out to introduce yourself or arranging a virtual coffee chat?**

6. Knowledge is power, and as you move into more advanced roles it is important to know your rights (e.g., laws regarding labor, racial discrimination, and sexual harassment). Attend a campus webinar on one of these topics or join an online community where you can safely ask questions and empower yourself and the staff around you. **Have you considered taking a self-assessment to gauge your knowledge on these topics, given that the landscape shifts quickly?**

7. Invest in self-care and pay attention to your mental health. Examples include setting and maintaining work–life balance, taking time away from the office, and/or seeking the support of a mental health professional. Remember that you are modeling behavior for those who report to you. **When was the last time that you took a mental health day?**

8. Reaching out for support can be a challenge for first-generation professionals, who tend to be self-reliant and independent. Remember: Asking for help does not mean that you are weak or incompetent. **How comfortable do you feel asking for help?**

9. Believe in yourself and the limitless possibilities! Even when you doubt yourself, ask for a title change or apply for a new position. Try something new or different, like joining a committee that will expand your network and increase your work awareness. **When was the last time you had a check in with your manager about your abilities and areas where you can stretch yourself for professional growth?**

References

Alcock, A., & Belluigi, D. Z. (2018). Positioning home for resilience on campus: First-generation students negotiate powerless/full conditions in south African higher education. *Education as Change, 22*(1), 1–28. http://www.scielo.org.za/pdf/eac/v22n1/07.pdf

Alessandria, K. P., & Nelson, E. S. (2005). Identity development and self-esteem of first-generation American college students: An exploratory study. *Journal of College Student Development, 46*(1), 3–12. https://doi.org/10.1353/csd.2005.0001

Anderson, E. C. (2006). If we want to boost retention and achievement, we need to work from student strengths, not weaknesses. *About Campus, 11*(4), 4–5.

Anderson, J. E., Guido-DiBrito, F., & Morrell, J. S. (2000). Factors that influence satisfaction for student affairs administrators. In L. S. Hagedorn (Ed.), *What contributes to job satisfaction among faculty and staff* (New Directions for Institutional Research, No. 105, pp. 99–110). Jossey-Bass. https://doi.org/10.1002/ir.10509

Azmitia, M., Sumabat-Estrada, G. S., Cheong, Y., & Covarrubias, R. (2018). "Dropping out is not an option": How educationally resilient first-generation students see the future. In C. R. Cooper & R. Seginer (Eds.), *Navigating pathways in multicultural nations: Identities, future orientation, schooling, and careers* (New Directions for Child and Adolescent Development, No. 160, pp. 89–100). Jossey-Bass.

Bardoel, E. A., Pettit, T. M., De Cieri, H., & McMillan, L. (2014). Employee resilience: An emerging challenge for HRM. *Asia Pacific Journal of Human Resources, 52*(3), 279–297. https://doi.org/10.1111/1744-7941.12033

Benight, C., & Cieslack, R. (2011). Cognitive factors in resilience: How self-efficacy contributes to coping with adversity. In S. M. Southwich, B. T. Litz, D. Charney, & M. J. Friedman (Eds.), *Resilience and mental health: Challenges across the lifespan* (pp. 30–44). Cambridge University Press.

Bourdieu, P. (1986). The forms of capital. In J. Richardson (Ed.), *Handbook of theory and research for the sociology of education* (pp. 241–258). Greenwood Press.

Burke, M. G., Dye, L., & Hughey, A. W. (2016). Teaching mindfulness for the self-care and well-being of student affairs professionals. *College Student Affairs Journal, 34*(3), 93–107. https://digitalcommons.wku.edu/csa_fac_pub/73

Clauss-Ehlers, C. S., & Wibrowski, C. R. (2007). Building educational resilience and social support: The effects of the educational opportunity fund program among first- and second-generation college students. *Journal of College Student Development, 48*(5), 574–584. https://doi.org/10.1353/csd.2007.0051

Coles, A. (2012). *The role of community-based organizations in the college access and success movement.* Pathways to College Network. https://www.ihep.org/wp-content/uploads/2014/06/uploads_docs_pubs_pcn_roleofcbo.pdf

Connor, K. M., & Davidson, J. R. (2003). Development of a new resilience scale: The Connor-Davidson resilience scale (CD-RISC). *Depression and Anxiety, 18*(2), 76–82. https://doi.org/10.1002/da.10113

Davis, D. M., & Hayes, J. A. (2011). What are the benefits of mindfulness? A practice review of psychotherapy-related research. *Psychotherapy, 48*(2), 198.

Franke, R., Hurtado, S., Pryor, J. H., & Tran, S. (2011). *Completing college: Assessing graduation rates at four-year institutions.* Higher Education Research Institute, Graduation School of Education & Information Studies, University of California, Los Angeles. http://heri.ucla.edu/DARCU/CompletingCollege2011.pdf

Gibbons, M. M. (2014). Addressing the needs of first-generation college students: Lessons learned from adults from low-education families. *Journal of College Counseling, 17*, 21–36.

Gordon, K. A. (1996). Resilient Hispanic youths' self-concept and motivational patterns. *Hispanic Journal of Behavioral Sciences, 18*(1), 63–73. https://doi.org/10.1177/07399863960181007

Guthrie, V. L., Woods, E., Cusker, C., & Gregory, M. (2005). A portrait of balance: Personal and professional balance among student affairs educators. *College Student Affairs Journal, 24*(2), 110–127. https://files.eric.ed.gov/fulltext/EJ956997.pdf

Helgeson, V. S., Reynolds, K. A., Siminerio, L. M., Becker, D. J., & Escobar, O. (2014). Cognitive adaptation theory as a predictor of adjustment to emerging adulthood for youth with and without type 1 diabetes. *Journal of Psychosomatic Research, 77*(6), 484–491. https://doi.org/10.1016/j.jpsychores.2014.09.013

Hirt, J. B., Schneiter, S. R., & Amelink, C. T. (2005). The nature of relationships and rewards for student affairs professionals at liberal arts institutions. *College Student Affairs Journal, 25*(1), 6–19. https://files.eric.ed.gov/fulltext/EJ957009.pdf

Hoffer, T. B. (2003). *Doctorate recipients from US universities.* NORC at the University of Chicago.

Horn, L. J., & Chen, X. (1998). *Toward resiliency: At-risk students who make it to college.* U.S. Government Printing Office.

Johnsrud, L. (1996). *Maintaining morale: A guide to assessing the morale of mid-level administrators and faculty.* College and University Personnel Association.

Liu, Y., Wang, Z., Zhou, C., & Li, T. (2014). Affect and self-esteem as mediators between trait resilience and psychological adjustment. *Personality and Individual Differences, 66,* 92–97.

Lopez, S. J., & Louis, M. C. (2009). The principles of strengths-based education. *Journal of College and Character, 10*(4). https://doi.org/10.2202/1940-1639.1041

Maddux, J. E. (Ed.). (2013). *Self-efficacy, adaptation, and adjustment: Theory, research, and application.* Springer Science & Business Media.

Margolis, E. (2001). *The hidden curriculum in higher education.* Routledge.

Moschetti, R. V., & Hudley, C. (2015). Social capital and academic motivation among first-generation community college students. *Community College Journal of Research and Practice, 39*(3), 235–251. https://doi.org/10.1080/10668926.2013.819304

Olson, J. (2014). Opportunities, obstacles and options: First-generation college graduates and social cognitive career theory. *Journal of Career Development, 41*(3), 199–217. https://doi.org/10.1177/0894845313486352

Orbe, M. P. (2008). Theorizing multidimensional identity negotiation: Reflections on the lived experiences of first-generation college students. In M. Azmitia, M. Syed, & K. A. Radmacher (Eds.), *The intersections of personal and social identities* (New Directions for Child and Adolescent Development, No. 120, pp. 81–95). Jossey-Bass.

Pike, G. R., & Kuh, G. D. (2005). First- and second-generation college students: A comparison of their engagement and intellectual development. *Journal of Higher Education, 76*(3), 276–300. https://doi.org/10.1080/00221546.2005.11772283

Reed, M., Maoddzwa-Taruvinga, M., Ndofirepi, E. S., & Moosa, R. (2019). Insights gained from a comparison of South African and Canadian first-generation students: The impact of resilience and resourcefulness on higher education success. *Compare: A Journal of Comparative International Education, 49*(6), 964–982. https://doi.org/10.1080/030579 25.2018.1479185

Rees, C. S., Breen, L. J., Cusack, L., & Hegney, D. (2015). Understanding individual resilience in the workplace: The international collaboration of workforce resilience model. *Frontiers in Psychology, 6*(73), 1–7. https://doi.org/10.3389/fpsyg.2015.00073

Rutter, M. (2007). Resilience, competence, and coping. *Child Abuse & Neglect, 31*(3), 205–209. https://10.1016/j.chiabu.2007.02.001

Schwarzer, R., & Warner, L. M. (2013). Perceived self-efficacy and its relationship to resilience. In S. Prince-Embury & D. H. Saklofske (Eds.), *Resilience in children, adolescents, and adults* (pp. 139–150). Springer.

Soria, K. M., & Stebleton, M. J. (2012). First-generation students' academic engagement and retention. *Teaching in Higher Education, 17*(6), 673–685.

Sostrin, J. (2016, August 8). The hidden curriculum of work. *Organizations and People*. https://www.strategy-business.com/blog/The-Hidden-Curriculum-of-Work?gko=b3cb3

Stephens, N. M., Fryberg, S. A., Markus, H. R., Johnson, C. S., & Covarrubias, R. (2012). Unseen disadvantage: How American universities' focus on independence undermines the academic performance of first-generation college students. *Journal of Personality and Social Psychology, 102*(6), 1178–1197. https://doi.org/10.1037/a0027143

Storlie, C. A., Mostade, S. J., & Duentas, D. (2016). Cultural trailblazers: Exploring the career development of Latina first-generation college students. *Career Development Quarterly, 64*(4), 304–317. https://doi.org/10.1002/cdq.12067

Tate, K. A., Caperton, W., Kaiser, D., Pruitt, N. T., White, H., & Hall, E. (2015). An exploration of first-generation college students' career development beliefs and experiences. *Journal of Career Development, 42*(4), 294–310. https://psycnet.apa.org/doi/10.1177/0894845314565025

Taylor, S. E., & Brown, J. D. (1988). Illusion and well-being: A social psychological perspective on mental health. *Psychological Bulletin, 103*(2), 193. https://psycnet.apa.org/doi/10.1037/0033-2909.103.2.193

Terry, D. J., Tonge, L., & Callan, V. J. (1995). Employee adjustment to stress: The role of coping resources, situational factors, and coping responses. *Anxiety, Stress & Coping, 8*(1), 1–24. https://doi.org/10.1080/10615809508249360

Vélez-Ibáñez, C. G., & Greenberg, J. B. (1992). Formation and transformation of funds of knowledge among U.S. Mexican households. *Anthropology & Education Quarterly, 23*(4), 313–335. https://doi.org/10.1525/aeq.1992.23.4.05x1582v

Warburton, E. C., Bugarin, R., & Nuñez, A. M. (2001). *Bridging the gap: Academic preparation and postsecondary success of first-generation students* (NCES 2001–153). U.S. Department of Education, National Center for Education Statistics. https://nces.ed.gov/pubs2001/2001153.pdf

Wildhagen, T. (2015). "Not your typical student": The social construction of the "first-generation" college student. *Qualitative Sociology, 38*(3), 285–303. https://doi.org/10.1007/s11133-015-9308-1

Yosso, T. J. (2005). Whose culture has capital? A critical race theory discussion of community cultural wealth. *Race Ethnicity and Education, 8*(1), 69–91. https://doi.org/10.1080/1361332052000341006

6

The Power of Community

The Importance of Professional Networks and Resources

SAMANTHA PAYTON AND BRANDI HEPHNER LABANC

This chapter starts with two stories. First up is Meaghan. Meaghan was attending a professional conference and discovered that the author of a publication she recently read and found useful was presenting. She wanted to meet this person and ask a few questions related to their shared research interests. She developed an introduction, carefully wrote out the questions she would like to ask, and mustered up the courage to introduce herself when she recognized him walking between program sessions. She called his name, Dr. Rainbow, a few times and finally caught his attention and introduced herself. Ten minutes later, as the conversation started winding down, he asked Meaghan why she kept calling him Dr. Rainbow, when his name was Dr. Reinbau.

Then there is Dominic. As a sophomore undergraduate student in business, Dominic was asked to provide a résumé for an internship interview. Dominic had heard of a résumé, but had no idea what a proper résumé should look like or what information it should include. Dominic had no idea who to turn to for direction and knew no one working in a business role. She didn't even know what information a résumé included. Unknowingly, as Dominic was worrying about how to figure out what a résumé really was, she was walking past the career development center within the College of Business. Dominic passed it twice daily.

For those of you who have found and continue to find networking intimidating, you might have cringed and felt sympathetic embarrassment when Meaghan discovered that she had called Dr. Reinbau by the wrong name. Or, in Dominic's case, you may have recalled feeling the panic and anxiety of navigating an intimidating business world where everyone but you seems to have their act together and know who to turn to or where to find resources. You might have even rationalized to yourself that these internal conflicts and challenges are exactly why you resist networking—why put yourself through the stress? Or, over time, you may have justified that your first "gen-ness" helped you to figure things out—that grit comes from forging your own path versus being disadvantaged. However, the reality is that the outcome of Meaghan's interaction would have been the same whether she made her mistake. In fact, it improved the outcome, as now Meaghan is a memorable interaction in a sea of perfectly executed introductions. In Dominic's case, although the experience would have been less arduous had she been directed to use the resources available to her, she researched how to write a résumé at the library and subsequently landed the internship.

Successful networking is about forming authentic connections between yourself and others and being directed to tap into resources that will support your goals. This is true wherever you are in your professional journey. If you have ever felt your first-generation status has been a barrier, it is time to start reframing that interpretation as your fresh approach and unique perspective acting as an advantage. As you move into the next phase of your professional career, be resolute in embracing the advantages of being first-generation. Where there have been missteps, take cues from earlier experiences and never be apologetic for asking questions and seeking support. After all, that is exactly what we ask our students to do all the time—be curious and reach out.

Even if You Think You Don't Need to Network, You Do

As first-generation professionals, we tend to share a few characteristics that make it harder to independently attack the task of networking with enthusiastic vigor. For one, we usually start our professional careers with a limited network that comprises proximal colleagues, instead of extended networks gained through familial or other legacy connections. To complicate the issue, familial or legacy relationships are not necessarily helpful or supportive. All student affairs professionals have been engaged in a conversation about explaining our work to parents, family members, or loved ones; this dialogue proves more complex for first-generation professionals. In fact, some first-generation professionals in higher education are initially discouraged by family members because they are perceived as "stuck in college" or family members felt their profession of choice does not pay well enough for a college graduate. Without the experience of attending college, it may be difficult for family members to engage in meaningful and supportive discussions about the work germane to first-generation professionals. These dynamics muddle first-generation professionals' journey and can render them feeling confused or guilty, and can certainly threaten professional retention and success. This is exactly why building a professional network is so critical to professional success.

Proximal connections are valuable for day-to-day tasks, but the length of these networks limits our breadth of knowledge. Specifically, by our very nature of being first-generation, we are socialized by those who have not experienced higher education or student affairs. To that end, we have limited or no opportunities to learn from those who have direct experience in the environment in which we find ourselves immersed. This is illustrated in Figure 6.1. The *x*-axis represents the universal knowledge pool; each connection is separated by a certain length that represents the distance from your current work environment.

Figure 6.1

An Analytical Perspective on Networking—Potential Knowledge/Skill Pool

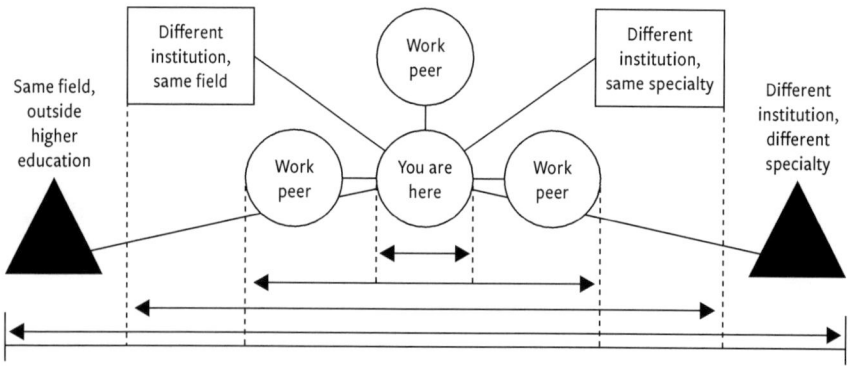

As Figure 6.1 demonstrates, proximal colleagues do contribute to your knowledge and skills pool; however, if you rely solely on these networks you can become too narrow in your professional development. Mid- and high-level positions in higher education require candidates to be visionary strategic thinkers with high competency in relational tasks. Developing this ability requires not only being an expert in your field, but also being versed in how other environments function (e.g., 4-year public versus 4-year private institutions) and the language of other specializations (e.g., counseling center direct client service versus counseling center triage), as well as the ability to communicate with and engage others in shared outcomes and goals. The appropriate networks are critical for this level of development. The networks must include more experienced individuals in positions similar to yours, but also professionals in the next level up positions. Networking with those in positions one step ahead of yours, or in the next position you seek, broadens your perspective and helps facilitate your professional growth.

First-generation professionals tend to heavily rely on self. We place responsibility for growth, development, and completion of tasks squarely on our own shoulders with little reliance on outside support. This is not surprising, as most of us learned this behavior during our undergraduate years. Because familial support and guidance during undergraduate tenure is limited or nonexistent, this forces first-generation students to rely on themselves to find, synthesize, and use information to their benefit. Though this character trait is a strength for first-generation professionals in terms of resilience, problem solving, and intrinsic motivation (see Chapter 5), it can create a challenge when it comes to networking and self-advocacy. We tend to resist networking by labeling it as a practice of manipulative and insincere favor trading, when in fact we should view it as the authentic, sincere development of a personal community that provides guidance, support, and information. In this way, first-generation professionals can view networking as an accumulation of navigational capital (Yosso, 2005) that allows them to not only succeed, but flourish, in complex and unfamiliar environments while maintaining the unique individual agency that defines us.

Ironically, even first-generation student affairs professionals (a self-proclaimed helping profession) are often resistant to the idea of asking others for guidance and assistance. In fact, we often feel like we have to prove ourselves among more experienced colleagues or pass ourselves off as being more knowledgeable than our colleagues about aspects of the higher education environment (even when these aspects are not a part of our job). The very nature of moving into mid-level or higher level positions requires one to delegate and rely on teams and committees to execute key initiatives. This managerial shift can truly challenge a first-generation professional who has too often relied on self in lieu of embracing the network of capable others. Sadly, these inclinations can lead to burnout and manifest themselves as poor management practices, such as micromanaging or overfunctioning.

Building a network is also paramount to increasing the volume of your voice in your chosen profession. How often have you read a research article or a professional journal and thought, "That wasn't my experience"? It is not uncommon for campus climate surveys to report staff feeling unheard or invisible when it comes to organizational decisions, nor is it uncommon for research to miss the valuable perspective of first-generation professionals. Building your network so that individuals in your field or organization are aware of your expertise and the topics that interest you will go a long way toward getting you those coveted committee invitations and prestigious research collaborations, where your experience can inform policy and the global community. Further, building networks yields support when you need it most, and allows you to create inroads whereby you can in turn support others.

Table 6.1

Three Forms of Professional Networking

	Operational	Personal	Strategic
Purpose of network	Completing day-to-day projects and tasks efficiently	Completing professional development, outreach, and referrals	Setting goals, planning strategically, and generating buy-in
Network compilation	Proximal colleagues and peers with whom you work consistently	Distal colleagues who satisfy current professional interests	Combination of proximal and distal colleagues who are perceived to be necessary for future planning and development
Professional benefit of network	Developing depth (expertise) specific to your field of work	Developing breadth of knowledge and skills related to your field of work	Developing a system of leverage that can be called on for support, guidance, and additional information (expertise)

Table 6.1 (modified from Ibarra & Hunter, 2007) summarizes the three types of networks that all professionals should actively develop throughout their careers. The majority of professionals will create operational networks organically as a function of their everyday work priorities. These networks primarily function to build expertise in your field of work and accomplish immediate tasks. However, focusing primarily on your operational network will inevitably lead you to perform sub optimally when placed in positions that require "big picture" thinking. These higher level positions will require more than just completing tasks as assigned and managing immediate crises following established protocols. You will need to use your personal and strategic networks to not only maintain efficiency but start asking questions related to the "why" and "how" of current and future operations. For example, you may have a colleague who continues to operate under outdated protocols because "that's how it's always been done," and they are an expert in that process. Compare this mentality to a colleague who continually asks "why are we doing it this way?" and seeks to update processes based on current best practices and research. The first colleague might have a strong operational network, but is clearly lacking the personal and strategic networks necessary to build vision. While this colleague might be an expert in their specific field, their narrow vision will inevitably cause them to be ineffective when assigned tasks that fall outside of their expertise.

Being a first-generation professional is challenging enough, but the intersectionality with other identities and socioeconomic status creates additional barriers. When discussing networking, it is not uncommon to hear people say, "It is not what you know, it is who you know." However, this country club mentality has the ability to immobilize some professionals. Chances are, as a first-generation professional moves into mid-level and higher level positions, this mentality will likely be more prevelant and more frequently encountered. Consider some of the efforts outlined in Table 6.2 to help the next generation of first-generation professionals in student affairs.

Table 6.2

How to Help a First-generation Student or Professional

Stop their fall	Many first-generation professionals fell into their position because no one talked to them about what it means to be a student affairs professional. Talk to your students about how their academic major relates and can contribute to the profession.
Empower	This applies to all students, not just those in higher education. Help them see their first-generation status as a strength, not a deficit. Help first-generation students effectively tell their story and position their lived experiences as advantages in their chosen profession.
Mentor	When a student expresses interest in higher education as an academic interest, work with them to prepare their application and interview day materials. The same applies to graduate students pursuing a terminal degree, or professional staff returning to the classroom.
Make connections	Invite first-generation graduate students and professionals into your networks. Invite people in versus waiting for them to ask. It is also appropriate to coach others on how to network, such as practicing introductions, reviewing introductory emails, and setting up meaningful conversations. When you introduce first-generation professionals to others in your network, do not be afraid to point out why they might need each other in their lives.
Make corrections	Call out destructive first-generation behavior. When you see a first-generation student or professional taking on more work than necessary, point it out and help them adjust. When you hear a first-generation individual question their worth, point it out and help them reframe.
Hire and promote	Having a first-generation perspective on staff brings a different perspective to policy making and professional practice. Actively and appropriately draw out the first-generation perspective to enrich your work. Likewise, be aware that some first-generation professionals will perpetually feel inadequate or see themselves as an imposter. Advocate and encourage them to take the next step professionally when they are ready. You will more than likely see that opportunity before they see it.

Although the student affairs profession aims to be highly inclusive, there is still room for improvement in our practices. If we look closely at our professional socialization, human resource practices, orientation, and mentoring, we can still identify embedded systemic bias that could limit first generation professionals. Within NASPA–Student Affairs Administrators in Higher Education, programs like the NASPA

Undergraduate Fellows Program are excellent ways to introduce under-represented professionals to the broader professional network, and NASPA's Alice Manicur Symposium and Mid-Managers Institute are prime opportunities for first-generation, mid-level managers. By participating in a fellowship or attending an institute, professionals get exposure to resources, network with more experienced professionals, and learn more about what skills and knowledge are needed to be successful in the field. Above all, these programs connect participants and attendees directly into the professional network. Beyond NASPA, the American Association of State Colleges and Universities and Harvard University offer an exceptional series of higher education leadership programs through the university's Graduate School of Education. Student affairs departments or divisions often endorse these types of programs, or similar efforts may be constructed on campus or regionally to facilitate the success of first-generation and underrepresented professionals.

Best Practices in Professional Networking

Building and maintaining a professional network takes effort. For first-generation professionals, this effort is heaviest at the front end because we usually do not possess familial or professional networks to jumpstart us. Once a newer professional is feeling established within their area of expertise and has connected to a professional network, they are typically promoted or looking for the next challenge. Once promoted, the existing matrix of support becomes less relevant; the professional often needs to start over and build a whole new network relevant to the new professional role. Sometimes those networks are connected or the resources are related, but the effort to expand on the current network is still much more daunting for the first-generation professional. There is no one-size-fits-all recipe for successful networking. However, the following list summarizes a few of the best practices to incorporate into your network development plan:

- Identify the community of practitioners that can be of most assistance to you.
- Connect and start the engagement/conversation with easy icebreakers. Don't try to sell yourself—you belong in this profession, too.
- Develop a memorable introduction that incorporates your identity, purpose, and values.
- Study the members of your professional area of practice and learn what they do and how it relates to your work; listen intently to what they have to say.
- Maintain a six degrees of separation map as you build your network.
- Engage fully with your network often; give and take equally.

Although much of networking involves in-person interaction, it is important to remember that technology facilitates so much of our working world, and thus should be leveraged to build effective networks. Be mindful, however, that networking is forming authentic connections, and that can be more challenging via email or on social media platforms. Ideally, technology can be used to initiate a relationship, and meaningful follow-up can then occur via phone conversations, video meetings, or in-person meetings at conferences or in other professional settings. No matter how you proceed with your network development plan, consider some of the strategies below as you navigate new professional spaces. These examples are also relevant to all stages of one's professional career.

Start the Conversation

The hardest part of starting the conversation is reading the environment to find your "in." The easiest scenario is finding a person or a community of professionals you wish to talk to one on one. Otherwise, the key is waiting for a lull in the group's conversation. This will be your opportunity to subtlety insert yourself and start a conversation. You can break the ice in several ways:

- If you are aware of a connection between yourself and this new contact, open with that. For example: *Good morning, Dr. Smith, my name is Dr. Sam Payton, and I believe we studied under the same mentor during graduate school.*
- Use what you know about the person to your advantage. How did you become aware of this individual? This will not only serve as an easy icebreaker, but also demonstrate to the individual that you find value in their work. For example: *Good morning, Dr. Smith, my name is Dr. Sam Payton, and I find your research into the psychological basis of undergraduate career choice incredibly fascinating.*
- If you have no connection to or prior knowledge of one's work, utilize professional or social networking forums to identify these connections and give you a point of entry when you have the opportunity to connect in person. You can also use an event, meeting, or conference to break the ice. For example:
  - On a social networking site or in a professional forum: *Dr. Smith, my name is Dr. Sam Payton, and I appreciated your recent post on LinkedIn discussing the importance of injecting a scholarly identity into student affairs practice.*
  - At an event/conference: *Good morning, Dr. Smith. My name is Dr. Sam Payton, and I recognize you from the earlier session. I am wondering what you thought about the argument that students are isolating themselves from university social events?*
- When all else fails, find the food or refreshments table. Making a statement about the food, size of the event, or meeting topic invites people to share their opinions, perceptions, and feelings. That engagement will usually seamlessly lead into introductions. For example:
  - Have you attended this event before?
  - What did you think of the meeting?
  - What do you think of the conference so far?

> ◆ I am happy they offered tea as well as coffee. Have you tried the Earl Grey with cream or sugar? It's like coffee without the jitters.

Develop a Memorable Introduction

"What do you do?" This question is common at networking events, meetings, and conferences. Think back to an instance when you were asked that question, or when you asked that question of a colleague. Did you or your colleague feel or appear uncomfortable when responding? Did the response appear to fall flat, or not progress the conversation forward? It is not uncommon for mid- to high-level professionals to fall flat with this response. When we are beginning our professional journey, we tend to focus our attention on questions such as the one presented above. We innocently do this as we are focused on getting that first job or making that first jump to mid-level. Once we make it though, this practice tends to get ignored and replaced by a title. However, potential colleagues will find it difficult to authentically connect with a title, regardless of the weight behind it. Building your social capital thus requires consistent attention to how you present your networking value to a potential colleague. Fortunately, with a few simple techniques, you can take your one-line response from flat and forgettable to powerful and memorable.

To get started, answer the question: What do you do? Without overthinking it, write out a one-sentence response. Now evaluate your response. Did you include your job title? Place of work? Number of years in your role? This type of response is common, but problematic. It is laden with facts, and facts rarely leave a lasting impression. For example, think back to what factors led you to choose the undergraduate institution you attended. Without searching, try to answer the following questions:

- What was the faculty to student ratio?
- What percentage of graduates successfully gained employment?
- What was your major program's national ranking?
- What was your institution's *USA Today* ranking?

Most likely, you were not able to answer the majority of those questions. Market research has consistently demonstrated that prospective students do not prioritize institutional facts when making their college choice (CollegeXpress & Carnegie Dartlet, 2019). Rather, students recall emotional factors such as how the campus felt when they visited, how receptive the faculty in their program were, or how beautiful the campus was. In other words, facts aren't memorable. If institutions answered the question "What do you do?" with facts, the prospective student might learn how many students are enrolled or how many graduated the previous year. This approach leaves the prospective students to interpret and assign the value of what they actually do for their students. Instead, institutions answer that question by describing the experience and the emotion of being a part of the community. This response speaks more directly to the question and conveys meaningful value to the prospective students.

Similarly, no value is conveyed by a job title or simple facts. When you take this limited approach, you give permission for a colleague or potential employer to interpret the response based on their own experiences and biases. Instead, you might include in your response that you have been in your position for 10 years. Some recipients of this additive information could value your tenure as loyalty; others could devalue this fact as an indication that you are stuck or are resistant to change. Either way, a fact-based response rarely leads to additional questions, which means your dialogue will be unproductive and your potential connection will hesitate to invest in your network. Instead, give those you are networking with a description of your work, your experiences, and the passion you hold for your professional role.

The key is to engage the person you want in your network by capturing their interest and clearly convey your value in 60 to 90 seconds. Luckily, this is easily achieved using a longitudinal formula and practice. To begin, complete the worksheet in Figure 6.2, developed by the chapter authors.

Figure 6.2

Develop a Memorable Introduction Worksheet

PRESENT

Whom do you serve? _____

_____

_____

_____

What do you do for those you serve? _____

_____

_____

_____

PAST

How do you directly contribute to the success of those you serve?

_____

_____

_____

_____

_____

_____

_____

FUTURE

How do you see your role growing or evolving? _____

_____

_____

_____

What do you need to accomplish this vision? _____

_____

_____

_____

Once you have carefully answered these questions, the hard part of creating your memorable introduction is complete. Now condense your response to each section of information (*present, past, future*) to one sentence.

In answering the *present* section of the worksheet, you are elevating your job title to an outcome-based statement that describes the emotional essence of what you do. For instance, "I am the director of research, assessment, and planning" turns into "I lead rigorous data collection and analysis in order to effectively tell the story of how staff, programs, and facilities in higher education contribute to the success of students."

For the *past* section, the goal is to share a concrete example to support your present section value statement. This example needs to be one you would enthusiastically elaborate on when additional questions are posed (which is the optimal outcome to your introductory statement). Take the following example: "For instance, I created an interactive heat map of our student union that displayed usage statistics such as percentage of time booked and who was using the various spaces so we could demonstrate empirically that the student union was the living room of the campus."

The *future* section is the critical part of your introduction. Your goal is to project that you are forward thinking and believe the person you are speaking to can aid in this vision as a collaborative partner. In other words, you are closing your introduction by directly engaging with your new colleague with an open-ended question. It is important to maintain the open-ended structure of the conversation, as a simple "Yes" or "No" can immediately end your dialogue prematurely. The following is an example: "I'm interested in including more experiential elements to this quantitative narrative; what elements would you suggest?"

To summarize, constructing this 60- to 90-second introduction is the capstone in your networking arch. Through this statement, you are demonstrating personal value and personal vision, and also hinting that you value the potential connection's opinions and expertise. According to Yosso (2005), this is a clear demonstration of your strong personal identity while also demonstrating navigational capital in the form of ideas and support. Because first-generation professionals also tend to suffer from imposter syndrome (see Chapter 2 of this book), constructing and consistently using this statement also reinforces your value to yourself. Finally, you can easily modify this statement for specific audiences. Simply change the success story example and modify your future vision and engaging question accordingly.

Maintain a Six Degrees of Separation Map

Six degrees of separation mapping is a popular sociological theory that hypothesizes that any two people in the world can be connected through an average number of six links or acquaintances (Zhang & Tu, 2009). This theory was further popularized by the trivia game Six Degrees of Kevin Bacon, during which a group of friends challenge each other to find the shortest number of links between a random Hollywood actor and Kevin Bacon. Since its inception, this theory has been consistently supported through empirical research, even translating to social media and web-based communication methods (Backstrom et al., 2012; Newman, 2001; Watts et al., 2002; Xiaohua, 2010; Zhang & Tu, 2009).

We are all connected through the small world phenomenon, which has gotten even smaller through social networking. This phenomenon was first supported by experiments conducted by Stanley Milgram (1967) in the 1960s that evaluated the average number of people required to connect Person A to Person B by asking individuals from Boston and Omaha to try and get a letter to a complete stranger in Boston. The catch was that they could use only personal acquaintances as intermediaries. Milgram's results concluded that the letters reached the target by exchanging hands an average of six times. This idea is profoundly encouraging for first-generation professionals embarking on building a network, as this theory suggests that you already possess a deep network, rich in social capital, that simply needs to be tapped. In other words, none of us are starting from square one. For mid- to high-level professionals, this also means that the network you already possess can be easily expanded. Theoretically, by evaluating just a few nodes on your professional network, you could easily double or triple your professional assets with minimal effort.

For instance, say you read something that really piques your interest, and you would like to connect with the author of that piece. You could email the author and introduce yourself and ask follow-up questions. However, first scanning the environment (e.g., know anyone on the reference list, know anyone at their institution, any known social media or professional forum connections) to determine a preexisting connection between yourself and the individual can help facilitate a more productive and meaningful introduction. Perhaps someone in your organization attended the same graduate program as the author, or even worked with the author. Though there is no existing taboo that restricts you from simply reaching out to that author to form a connection, you can skip several introductory steps and begin a more authentic collaboration by moving through an intermediary joint connection. After all, most of us have experienced a colleague asking on behalf of another (unknown colleague) to help that individual with a project or provide insight. For instance, colleagues of a vice president might ask the senior leader to meet with a colleague seeking a vice presidency. It is not a stretch to assume that we jumped to provide that support, even without prior socialization with that peer, because we understand the power of the network and how shared knowledge makes us all better professionals. A six degrees of separation map serves the function of a "friend-of-a-friend" support network.

Creating a physical map allows you to visualize that journey. The following exercise will help you get started. Begin by making two lists. Include in the first those individuals with whom you would like to form a network. Include in the second those individuals you consider to be in your current network. These lists need not be comprehensive, as you will consistently build these out over time.

Figure 6.3

Six Degrees of Separation Map

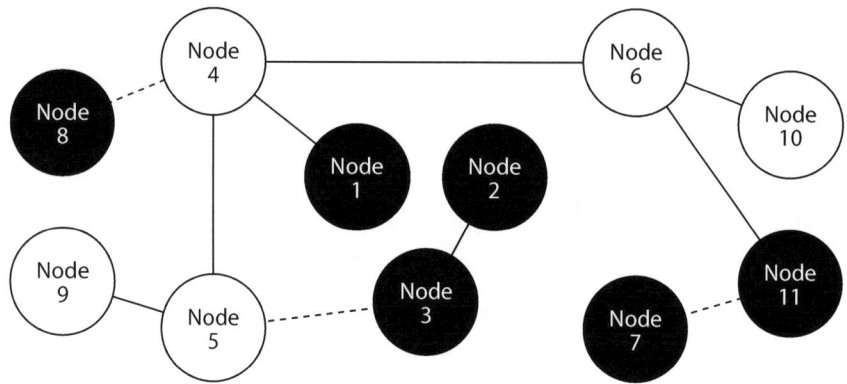

For each person with whom you would like to network, investigate their background. Who advised their graduate research? With whom have they published? With whom do they currently work within their office? Map each individual as a node on a network map, and use lines to connect nodes that have interacted with each other (see Figure 6.3 as an example). Customize your map to identify types of connections. For example, solid lines could represent mentor-mentee and coworker connections, and dashed lines could represent collaboration on published research. Light nodes could represent those with whom you wish to connect, while dark nodes represent your current connections. Use this map to continually remind yourself that you are indeed connected to a diverse and rich pool of colleagues that have the potential to offer substantial support throughout your career.

Table 6.3

Tips to Try at Your Next Conference

Make a memorable business card: Make it impossible for connections to forget you by adding a photo of yourself to your business cards. Connections will be able to associate your face with your name.
Engage in follow-up via social media: Use that stack of business cards you collected to find your connections on social media (Twitter, LinkedIn, Facebook, Instagram, etc.). Make that casual connection and use those feeds to capitalize on similarities.
Create an informative name tag: Change up your badge registration from your name and university to your name and category of research. This one strategy will greatly increase the probability of others identifying you as a potential connection.
Volunteer at a conference: By volunteering, not only will you be giving back to the event, but this is the easiest way to meet people at a conference, because it is literally your job to engage with the attendees. Use this to your advantage.

Use Your Network

It is important to remember that networking does not necessarily mean constantly building new connections. A massive network of individuals you have met once at a conference will offer no benefits to your professional development if you do not cultivate those relationships. In the realm of networking, quality will always trump quantity. After all, it becomes increasingly difficult to utilize a connection if enough time has passed that they no longer remember you and your common interests. The more intentional and authentic you are as you develop a professional relationship, the more likely that individual will connect you to meaningful relationships within their own network. The more meaningful that relationship becomes, the wealthier you become with regard to social capital.

The easiest way to maintain connections is to make it clear at your initial meeting how and when you will contact them. Make sure you follow up on this promise. A good approach is to establish quarterly phone/video meetings and then an annual in-person meeting at a professional conference. Be sure you thoughtfully plan for these meet-ups and do not waste your colleague's time. Also, ask key individuals in your network to review your critical work products or résumé as it is updated. These touchpoints will help develop your relationships, your contacts will learn more about you and your abilities, and you will learn what your contacts think about the profession and your shared work. Another technique is to develop reconnection triggers, or reminders, for the colleagues within your network. These triggers are based on your personal knowledge of and your shared interests with each connection. For instance, if one of your connections was built on shared research interests, set up an annotated reminder on your network map, business card, email, and so on, to send along to your connection articles or data relevant to those interests. That will not only maintain your visibility in terms of your network's working memory, but will reinforce your shared interests, which raises your value.

It is also important to selectively attend to your connections' special events, achievements, milestones, and professional development, where possible. This fosters the impression that you value the relationship you are building, which extends beyond simply developing a resource. For instance, if you notice that your colleague has been awarded a recog-nition or appointed to a board, send an email or card to congratulate them, thank them for their service, and reiterate why they are important to you. Or, if a colleague is presenting at a conference or hosting a recep-tion, stop by to show your support. Simple gestures recapitulate the very core of networking. Networking is the formation and cultivation of authentic connections between you and others. The more genuine you are when networking, the greater value you will receive from the process.

Postscript

The authors invited fellow first-generation professionals to sit with them and discuss their experiences as a catalyst for writing this chapter. The conversation was cathartic and inspiring as we collectively laughed and empathized with familiar and shared experiences despite our very different identities and professional pathways. From these conversations, we were all shocked at how many first-generation professionals were holding leadership roles in the student affairs division. At the end of the conversation, the authors posed the following question: What advice would you offer fellow first-generation professionals? The answers are depicted in Table 6.4.

Table 6.4
Advice From First-generation Professionals for Their Peers

Never question your worth.	Maybe you work at a private, elite institution or a Power Five public institution, yet you attended a regional, midsize college. Remember, you are where you are meant to be (they hired you!) and your institution needs your perspective to enrich the student experience.
Embrace the freedom.	The nice thing about being a first-generation professional is that there is no legacy to follow or specific loyalty (unless it is your own). You can work your whole career at your alma mater or move around the country to expand your experiences. The pathway is limitless and that freedom is special.
Your first-generation status is your superpower.	You have survived by adapting, and higher education needs adaptable leadership now more than ever. First-generation professionals are more comfortable in the uncomfortable than their counterparts. Lead the way because student affairs needs your adaptability more than ever right now!
Your instincts matter.	In general, first-generation professionals are hardworking, brave, and gritty; they prioritize becoming experts in their area of responsibility. Never lose that instinct, because it is your genius. Today, it is too easy to be caught up in our frenetic world, but first-generation professionals tend to slow down and work thoroughly and methodically. We are built for the marathon, not the sprint.
Trust is essential.	Maybe you have survived by relying on yourself, but seasoned professionals are your allies. You must trust yourself enough to be vulnerable and trust others. Take other professionals up on their offer to connect or assist you. It is perfectly fine for them to take that responsibility and for you to benefit from their network and experiences.

Questions for Reflection

1. As you develop professionally (e.g., acquiring new hard and soft skills, producing research and publications, becoming more of a voice in your profession), how should you concurrently evolve both the composition of your network as well as your networking strategies?

2. At this point in time, what do you want to focus on for your professional development? With that in mind, is your current network sufficiently composed of colleagues who can aid in this development? Are there individuals you could add to support your sustained development in these areas?

3. Identify your top five professional connections. How are you maintaining those relationships? What can you do to cultivate those relationships in an authentic and meaningful way?

4. When you reflect on your current network, are your connections mostly internal (or proximal) peers? Do they mostly work in your field of practice and at similar institutions? What are some areas of your network that you can expand (or diversify) to increase your social capital?

5. Reflect on your journey thus far. Regarding networking, what might you have done differently? What do you wish you had known? What did you do well? How can you ensure that other first-generation professionals learn from this wisdom?

References

Backstrom, L., Boldi, P., Rosa, M., Ugander, J., & Vigna, S. (2012). Four degrees of separation. In *WebSci '12: Proceedings of the 4th Annual ACM Web Science Conference* (pp. 31–42). Association for Computing Machinery. https://doi.org/10.1145/2380718.2380723

CollegeXpress & Carnegie Dartlet. (2019, November 21). *Student insights report.* http://www.Carnegiedartlet.com/cxreport

Ibarra, H., & Hunter, M. L. (2007, January). How leaders create and use networks. *Harvard Business Review.* https://hbr.org/2007/01/how-leaders-create-and-use-networks

Milgram, S. (1967). The small world problem. *Psychology Today, 1*(1), 60–67.

Newman, M. E. J. (2001). The structure of scientific collaboration networks. *Proceedings of the National Academy of Sciences of the United States of America, 98*(2), 404–409. https://doi.org/10.1073/pnas.98.2.404

Watts, D. J., Dodds, P. S., & Newman, M. E. J. (2002). Identity and search in social networks. *Science, 296*(5571), 1302–1305. https://doi.org/10.1126/science.1070120

Xiao-hua, K. (2010). A social networking services system based on the "six degrees of separation" theory and damping factors. In *Proceedings of the 2010 Second International Conference on Future Networks* (pp. 438–441). IEEE Computer Society. https://doi.org/10.1109/ICFN.2010.22

Yosso, T. J. (2005). Whose culture has capital? A critical race theory discussion of community cultural wealth. *Race Ethnicity and Education, 8*(1), 69–91. https://doi.org/10.1080/1361332052000341006

Zhang, L., & Tu, W. (2009). Six degrees of separation in online society. *Distribution, 3*(12), 1–5.

7

Empowerment
Through Mentoring

Robin M. Williamson

S tudies on the success of professionals in the workplace have shown that mentorship plays a crucial role. However, what impact does mentorship have on those who may not have had access or exposure to many professionals within their desired career field? Eesley and Wang (2014) found that mentorship has a positive effect on those individuals who may not have contact with entrepreneurial role models in their previous experiences. Prior to any college experience, first-generation students may not know about the field of student affairs. They may have difficulty finding student affairs professionals as career role models because they may not be aware of the field. When first-generation students become colleagues, their exposure to student affairs professionals becomes even more critical regarding their professional and personal development. As first-generation professionals grow and develop their portfolios, mentorship is critical for their professional development and short-, mid-, and long-term success.

Defining Mentoring

Mentoring is a highly personal experience and is defined differently by individuals. For the purposes of this chapter, *mentoring* is defined as a learning experience meant to transform both parties within the relationship (Daloz, 1986; Haley et al., 2015). A mentoring relationship can be a powerful tool for the development and advancement of the higher education professional. As practitioners move through the various stages of their careers, assuming the roles of both mentee and mentor invariably contribute to the progression of one's mastery of skills and professional knowledge.

Carpenter's (2003) three stages of professional development—formative, application, and additive—can also be applied to the mentor relationship. The formative stage occurs during graduate school or the beginning of one's career. The application stage usually occurs during the first few years of one's career. This is when one expands their knowledge of what it means to be a professional in their field. Those in the formative stage typically serve as mentees in a mentoring relationship. Depending on professional development, those in the application stage may have a mentee as well as a mentor. The additive stage does not typically have a set time in a career path but is characteristic of a mid-level position in higher education. Many professionals at this level have a mentor and a mentee. Higher education professionals in the additive stage generally find ways to improve the field beyond their campuses (Haley et al., 2015). Mentoring up and coming professionals is a way to improve the field of student affairs. Although anyone can serve as a mentor at any point in their career, it is a hallmark of those in the additive stage.

Mentoring can be prescribed or spontaneous. For example, many graduate programs or divisions of student affairs assign new members mentors to help them transition into their new role and the institutional community. Although assigned mentors have a meaningful and purposeful role, the focus of this chapter is the spontaneous type of mentoring: the unplanned connections between a mentee looking for an opportunity to continue growth and development and a mentor who not only has the ability to assist in the mentee's growth but also has the desire and capacity to learn from this relationship.

Exploration of Mentorship Compared With Other Kinds of Relationships

Many individuals enter the field of student affairs through a graduate program in higher education or related program of study. During that time, the student may get paired with a peer mentor, a faculty advisor, a thesis sponsor, or a graduate assistantship supervisor. Once in a full-time position, an individual may have a campus-assigned mentor, a human resources representative, a union advocate, or at least one supervisor. Considering all the ways campus communities onboard and retain talent, it is worth exploring the different types of professional relationships, especially for mid-level professionals.

New professionals in many industries seek out sponsors. Student affairs is no different, even if the sponsor role is not as formalized or structured. Baumgarten (n.d.) stated that sponsors are focused on propelling their protégé's career success. Mentors, on the other hand, assist in crafting their mentee's career vision. The sponsorship relationship allows for a more experienced and senior staff person to use their power, authority, influence, and professional networks to advance the career of the protégé. "In short, mentors advise you and sponsors advocate *for you*" (Baumgarten, n.d., para. 2).

As I prepared to leave a position to move closer to my partner, my supervisor quickly became my sponsor. It was the first time in my career that I was moving without a job and without a professional network already in place. My sponsor took the time to reach out to her network of peers to see if she knew anyone at a school within a 50-mile radius of my new home. When she did find connections, she was quick to email them and let them know I was moving to the area and in search of a position, and to electronically introduce me to these peers. It was extremely helpful to cultivate a strong professional network or colleagues and peers in my new hometown, and I eventually secured a position.

Role models are also important for first-generation student affairs professionals. For many first-generation students, a role model is what first sparks their interest in a student affairs career. A role model is someone an individual greatly respects and admires. Because individuals usually see their role model as highly successful, they may imitate the role model's behaviors to achieve the same type of success (Cheprasov, 2017). This type of relationship may or may not include a personal connection between the individual and their role model. In contrast, the mentoring relationship, although it involves a certain level of role modeling, is combined with personal relationship, guidance, and support to drive the mentee's success. Role models and mentors who have identities that match or complement the identities of their proteges can have powerful effects. Lockwood and Kunda (1997) found that their study participants were positively affected by a career-matched role model, and mismatched role models had no effect on participants. Role models who share at least one identity, such as gender, can be valuable in encouraging people when that identity may not be in the majority in a group setting (Rosenthal et al., 2013).

A supervisor is responsible for ensuring their employees have the knowledge, training, and other necessary resources to successfully complete their job responsibilities. A supervisor, however, is not inherently responsible for serving as a sponsor, role model, or mentor for their employees. Seasoned professionals should provide a level of supervision that allows employees to feel integrated into the office and on campus, feel confident in their level of support, and receive timely feedback on successes in addition to areas for growth. This kind of supervisor, known as a synergistic supervisor, has a tremendous impact on retaining professionals in any given field (Pittman & Foubert, 2016). As one progresses through their own career path, one should also identify and develop skills and capacities to be the type of supervisor, sponsor, role model, or mentor that empowers others. As one transitions from a new to mid-level professional, self-awareness and professional development are important factors in this evolution.

Finding and Developing a Mentoring Relationship

Mentoring relationships are complex and personal, and take time and effort to develop. These relationships are rooted in mutual respect and trust and are cultivated over a period of time. Although opportunities abound to meet and interact with colleagues on campus, finding a mentor can be an overwhelming task for any professional, especially a first-generation professional who may never have been exposed to the idea of mentoring. So where does one begin to find a mentor? As previously mentioned, institutions may assign a mentor to newly hired professionals, but usually that role involves housekeeping-focused tasks such as showing the new staff member around campus, making introductions, and being available for general questions. These individuals may carry the superficial title of "mentor"; however, true mentoring goes much deeper.

Zachary (2000) wrote that the primary purpose of mentoring relationships is learning, and that the mentoring relationship should focus on a learner-centered paradigm. In a learner-centered mentoring relationship, "wisdom is not passed from an authoritarian teacher to a supplicant student, but is discovered in a learning relationship in which both stand to gain a greater understanding of the workplace and the world" (Aubrey & Cohen, 1995, p. 161). In this partnership model, there is a shared sense of responsibility for both the relationship and the stated goals and outcomes (Zachary, 2000). Finding a mentor to invest the time and energy needed for professional growth can be a challenge for the first-generation professional, but there are several avenues through which this can be achieved.

Both formal and informal mentoring relationships can be found in professional organizations. Such organizations offer networking and mentoring opportunities to connect with established professionals in their chosen field of study. For both new and continuing professionals, involvement in these organizations assists in their career advancement and expands their network of community beyond their home institution (Rizzolo et al., 2015). Professional organizations also provide various mentoring opportunities, both formal (assigned) and informal (organic). These professional mentors can offer their mentees thoughtful input, guide their leadership development, and provide them access to professional expertise that may not be available within their home institution (Vess, 2014).

Professional organizations also provide new and continuing professionals an opportunity to engage in research and present at national and regional conferences. Conference presentations are often the first step to publication, an important part of professional development, and provide an opportunity to create and sustain relationships with mentors in the field (Vess, 2014). This is especially important for women and professionals of color, who may find their home institutions lacking in diversity and seek to find mentors and opportunities specifically related to their needs.

Although it is often easier for new professionals to find a mentor, it is imperative that mid-level professionals continue to seek out mentoring relationships. For example, as I transitioned to a mid-level position, I realized that there were still many areas in which I needed to develop, including spending the time and energy to fully grow and flesh out my vision for my career path. In my career, I had the great opportunity to hold multiple positions at one institution over the course of 15 years. As such, I sought out mentors who had also held multiple roles at the same institution. I also attended institutes and conferences that helped me understand the profession and how to successfully navigate the field. I also found sponsors who helped me find avenues to develop skills and competencies outside of my mid-level position's responsibilities. Through the encouragement of my mentors and support of my sponsors, I volunteered to be on many campus committees, when time and work permitted. These activities enabled me to expand my network as well as my portfolio.

Preparing for Opportunities and Challenges in the Mentoring Relationship

Although the term *mentoring* is used as a broad description of the relationship between a designated mentor and mentee, the individual experiences within each mentoring relationship are based on the narratives each participant brings to the relationship, as well as each participant's individual personality and world view. The personalities of the mentor and mentee, and how well they are matched or even mismatched, are perhaps the most significant indicators of the success or failure of the relationship (Hayes & Koro-Ljungberg, 2011). Both inside and outside influences can create contexts in which the mentoring partnership struggles to find its footing from the beginning or derails a successful mentoring relationship years into the process. Both the mentor and the mentee should at the outset work to create a shared understanding of the expectations for the relationship and the values that will guide the relationship moving forward. As the relationship evolves, these parameters should be revisited and renegotiated if needed (Hayes & Koro-Ljungberg, 2011).

Mentees may have unrealistic expectations for their mentors and the multiple roles they are expected to play in their lives (Zachary, 2000). Mentees may confuse the ideas of role model, supervisor, and mentor and unconsciously assign more than one role to a mentor, creating tension and pressure on the mentor to be an all-encompassing source of support for the mentee. Additionally, depending how the relationship was developed (formally or informally), there may be a power dynamic that needs to be acknowledged and addressed. The mentee and mentor should see this power dynamic as an opportunity to define the relationship and roles and assign meaning based on a shared construction of the terms based on the individual mentoring relationship (Hayes & Koro-Ljungberg, 2011). For example, one of my mentors was originally my supervisor in my first professional position. My mentor/supervisor and I took the time to talk about the power dynamic. It was extremely helpful to be able to delineate between job expectations and responsibilities and mentoring suggestions. One tactic I like to use in my mentoring relationships is to create an agreement form for both parties. Many templates available online can be adapted to fit this need. By having something in writing, both parties have clear definitions and understanding of each other's expectations. It can also be a guideline to determine when to adjust or end the mentoring relationship. For example, if my mentee and I have met all of the expectations and goals set forth in our agreement, I take the opportunity to explore whether we want to continue with a formal mentor relationship. Of course, I will always be available for advice and coaching, but my mentee may be ready for another type of relationship with someone else. I have had mentees look to find a new mentor for a variety of reasons, such as they relocated to another city or state and wanted to still have a chance to meet face to face with their mentor. Mentees have also changed jobs and have wanted to find a new mentor in that particular field if I have not had experience in that area. A good mentor will support the needs of their mentee and vice versa.

Even with well-defined relationship parameters, situations may arise in which the expectations fall short or the relationship experiences pitfalls. Roles may be taken for granted; roles and the relationship lines may get blurred, causing confusion; mentors or mentees may become unfocused or preoccupied with personal or professional conflicts, resulting in a withdrawal from the relationship; or a mentor may inadvertently cross a line and undermine their mentee's development (Zachary, 2000). I have seen mentoring relationships end when mentors or mentees have forgotten to adhere to their mentoring agreement. For example, a mentee uses their mentoring relationship with a mentor to leverage certain advantages in the workplace. I have seen someone use their personal relationship with their mentor to get a preferred office space or time off. Using the name and position of the mentor created conflict within the office and caused the mentor to appear to be playing favorites amongst the staff. Identifying these incidences as they occur and reaching common ground to resolve them is paramount to the success of a mentoring relationship. For mentees who feel their mentors may have blurred lines, it can lead to an uncomfortable situation and a strain on the mentoring relationship. Having a written, formal agreement may help mentors and mentees address these situations when they may arise.

With a formal agreement in place, the mentee as well as the mentor can suggest regular status reports on desired goals and expectations. Typically, I write a monthly review of the agreement as one of my formal expectations. By having clearly written expectations, it can take the pressure off both parties when any issues may arise. The formal agreement can be a reminder and a touchstone for when something goes awry. If an issue is not able to wait until a regularly scheduled review, either party should suggest an immediate review of expectations. For example, I recently had a situation where my mentor interrupted me multiple times in a meeting I was leading. I was uncomfortable and upset. Instead of waiting until our scheduled meeting, I asked if we could speak the next day. I asked my mentor if he had any feedback for me regarding my performance as the meeting leader. By asking for feedback, it signaled that I was invested in his professional insight and guidance, but also allowed me to state why I was seeking immediate feedback. It ended up being one of our best conversations.

Impact of Mentoring Relationships

Although new professionals compose up to a quarter of all student affairs staff, they tend to leave the field within their first 5 years of employment (Pittman & Foubert, 2016). When the employment pipeline loses many of its newly trained staff within the first few years of hiring, the loss of talent has a tremendous impact on the profession. Most studies focus on the impact of mentoring on individuals during their first year of graduate school or professional work. Considering how many new professionals leave the field of student affairs, it is important to reflect on the impact mentoring can play for the mid-level professional.

By the time a new professional masters the expectations of their new position, it is usually time for the next job search. For most higher education professionals, that typically means moving offices and departments, if not moving to another institution, city, or state. A mentor can be extremely helpful during the job search process, but is also extremely critical for the success of the mentee as they move into mid-level positions. As a higher education professional advances in their career, specific skills and competencies begin to become more significant for their long-term success, such as supervisory, budgeting, and human resources experience (Burkard et al., 2005). These skills and competencies may not even be gained or developed in an entry-level position. This can pose a huge disadvantage as entry-level professionals vie for competitive mid-level positions, such as assistant or associate director, that may require the supervision of professional staff, oversight of million-dollar budgets, and other high-level responsibilities.

When thinking about possibilities to expand one's portfolio in order to be a competitive candidate for mid-level positions, a review of Yosso's (2005) cultural wealth model can be extremely helpful (see Chapter 2 for further discussion). The six forms of capital can empower the first-generation professional to focus on means and avenues that can help lessen or even eliminate any disadvantage. As a mentee looks to advance in their career, they may not have had direct experience with certain criteria for a sought out position. Using Yosso's cultural wealth model as a lens to review a résumé or curriculum vitae, a mentor can help a mentee identify transferrable skills or experiences that would be appropriate for the desired position. For example, an institution searching for a new position may want someone who has a strong history of creating inclusive environments for students and other campus stakeholders. By reflecting on one's navigational capital skills, the candidate can clearly articulate and demonstrate methods and experiences that connected underrepresented and/or vulnerable populations with the goals of their current office and institution. If a job posting calls for a candidate to collaborate, network, or fundraise, a mentor can help their mentee identify ways to articulate their experiences that met those functions. By reflecting on social capital skills, a mentee can convey how they have connected students or the institution with necessary resources. Although a mentor may not be able to add specific opportunities to a professional profile, they may be able to assist their mentee in identifying competencies in addition to helping the mentee recognize their experiences in different contexts and with different lenses, such as through the lens of the cultural wealth model. A mentor may also be able to suggest comparable experiences to develop transferable skills in addition to coach the mentee on how to approach a supervisor to gain opportunities to cultivate in these skills.

Conclusion

A mentoring relationship can be extremely helpful in all stages of a professional's career. Mentoring is a transformative experience for both the mentor and the mentee. Through clearly predetermined and defined expectations, the mentor relationship can lead to many wonderful encounters for both parties. Mentors and mentees can choose to attend a professional meeting or conference together. Through these shared events, they can expand each other's professional networks as well as professional knowledge. Mentors and mentees can expand their comprehension of certain topics through book or article discussions. They can involve each other in work presentations or projects, as appropriate, in order to learn from as well as provide feedback to each other. Mentors can help identify strengths as well as gaps in job experiences for their mentees. They can also help their mentees identify other professional sources of support, such as role models or sponsors. Mentoring is not only a wonderful way for professionals to grow and develop, but it can also be a powerful tool to help one advance in their career.

Questions for Reflection

1. When entering into a mentoring relationship, reflect on whether this mentor can also be a sponsor.
2. Discuss your personal vision by answering the following question: What would you like to be remembered for over the next few years?
3. What keeps you up at night regarding your position?
4. Who is your mentor now? What are you developing through that relationship related to your next career steps? What do you need to develop through the relationship?

References

Aubrey, R., & Cohen, P. M. (1995). *Working wisdom: Timeless skills and vanguard strategies for learning organizations*. Jossey-Bass.

Baumgarten, M. (n.d.). *The key role of sponsorship*. https://inclusion.slac.stanford.edu/sites/inclusion.slac.stanford.edu/files/The_Key_Role_of_a_Sponsorship_for_Diverse_Talent.pdf

Burkard, A. W., Cole, D., Ott, M., & Stoflet, T. (2005). Entry-level competencies of new student affairs professionals: A Delphi study. *NASPA Journal, 42*(3), 283–309. https://doi.org/10.2202/1949-6605.1509

Carpenter, D. S. (2003). Professionalism. In S. R. Komives & D. Woodard, Jr. (Eds.), *Student services: A handbook for the profession* (4th ed., pp. 573–592). Jossey-Bass.

Cheprasov, A. (2017, December 29). *Role model vs. mentor: Compare and contrast* [Video]. Study.com. https://study.com/academy/lesson/role-model-vs-mentor-compare-contrast.html

Daloz, L. (1986). *Effective teaching and mentoring*. Jossey-Bass.

Eesley, C., & Wang, Y. (2014). The effects of mentoring in entrepreneurial career choice. *SSRN Electronic Journal*. http://funginstitute.berkeley.edu/wp-content/uploads/2014/09/Chuck_Eesley_Paper1.pdf

Haley, K., Jaeger, A., Hawes, C. & Johnson, J. (2015). Going beyond conference registration: Creating intentional professional development for student affairs educators. *Journal of Student Affairs Research and Practice, 52*(3), 313–326. https://doi.org/10.1080/19496591.2015.1050034

Hayes, S., & Koro-Ljungberg, M. (2011). Dialogic exchanges and the negotiation of differences: Female graduate students' experiences of obstacles related to academic mentoring. *The Qualitative Report, 16*(3), 682–710. https://nsuworks.nova.edu/tqr/vol16/iss3/4

Lockwood, P., & Kunda, Z. (1997). Superstars and me: Predicting the impact of role models on the self. *Journal of Personality and Social Psychology, 73*, 91–103. https://doi.apa.org/doi/10.1037/0022-3514.73.1.91

Pittman, E. C., & Foubert, J. D. (2016). Predictors of professional identity development for student affairs professionals. *Journal of Student Affairs Research and Practice, 53*(1), 13–25. https://doi.org/10.1080/19496591.2016.1087857

Rizzolo, S., DeForest, A. R., DeCino, D. A., Strear, M., & Landram, S. (2015). Graduate student perceptions and experiences of professional development activities. *Journal of Career Development, 43*(3), 195–210. https://doi.org/10.1177/0894845315587967

Rosenthal, L., Levy, S., London, B., Lobel, M., & Bazile, C. (2013). In pursuit of the MD: The impact of role models, identity compatibility, and belonging among undergraduate women. *Sex Roles, 68*(7–8), 464–473. https://doi.org/10.1007/s11199-012-0257-9

Vess, L. (2014). The role of the PSA in graduate student training and professional development. *The American Sociologist, 45*(2), 271–273. https://doi.org/10.1007/s12108-014-9215-z

Yosso, T. J. (2005). Whose culture has capital? A critical race theory discussion of community cultural wealth. *Race Ethnicity and Education, 8*(1), 69–91. https://doi.org/10.1080/1361332052000341006

Zachary, L. J. (2000). *The mentor's guide: Facilitating effective learning relationships*. Jossey-Bass.

PART III

Career Paths

8

First-generation Graduates in Mid-Level Career Transitions

AINSLEY CARRY

My story represents the highs and lows that many first-generation graduates face in mid-level careers. Neither of my parents had more than a high-school education, yet they believed in the value of hard work and education for their children. My three siblings and I attended public schools while our parents worked from morning until night to provide a home and put food on the table. Intellectual engagement at home was limited to what we watched on television; neither of our parents spent time doing much more than working. None of my siblings went to college, and I went because influential teachers and coaches encouraged me to. In college, I struggled due to inadequate academic preparation from my public school education. My parents and siblings were supportive, but they did not know how to advise me in college. I did not know what questions to ask or which pitfalls to avoid. I made mistakes typical of first-generation college students: poor financial planning, taking the wrong classes for my major, accepting more student loans than necessary, changing my major and wasting a year of coursework, not taking advantage of career development services and experiences (e.g., internships, practicums), and not building a personal or professional network. By graduation, I understood more about managing money in college, selecting courses, and interacting with professors. Although these lessons were costly and time-consuming, they were invaluable for my future career. Graduating from college only partially prepared me for the world of work; more meaningful lessons came from real-world experiences.

I made all the mistakes first-generation graduates make in the workplace. I accepted employment outside my field of study and below my qualifications. I focused on "getting a job" to pay bills rather than building a career. I did not benefit from parents or siblings who could advise me through the employment market or salary negotiations. Yet, my experience as a first-generation college student and graduate prepared me for challenges I would face later in my mid-level career transitions. My confidence grew in understanding how to leverage my experiences outside and inside the classroom. Although these discoveries alone were not enough to avoid every misstep, I recovered from mistakes because of my resilience. My experience as a first-generation graduate helped me develop skills I would apply throughout my professional career—using these transferable skills to achieve career success.

First-generation Students

The research is clear: First-generation students and their parents face many challenges. In college, students typically have difficulty navigating the admissions process (Choy, 2001; Horn & Nunez, 2000); getting socially and academically acclimated (Chen & Carrol, 2005; Jehangir, 2009; Stieha, 2010); and understanding faculty expectations (Collier & Morgan, 2008). In general, first-generation college students face unique financial challenges: they lack knowledge about how to pay for college (Kabaci & Cude, 2015), they come from lower socioeconomic backgrounds (Thayer, 2000), and they face challenges trying to pay for college (Thayer, 2000). As a result, they have lower graduation rates than their non-first-generation peers (Lohfink & Paulsen, 2005) and have more debt upon graduation. First-generation graduates start their careers in lower-paying jobs and spend more years earning wages below their qualifications, "thus attaining a lower return on their educational investment" (Hirudayaraj & McLean, 2017, p. 103). The loss of income from underemployment totals millions when compounded over a lifetime.

Families of first-generation college students are proud of their student's accomplishments but knowingly have limited capacity to provide logistical help during the academic experience. Hirudayaraj and McLean (2017) interviewed first-generation graduates about career support from their families. Interviewees acknowledged their families provided minimal career-oriented conversations while growing up and lacked social networks to launch their careers. The researchers discovered the difference in "the support they as students received from significant adults in their families" versus their peers with college-educated parents (p. 96). They also recognized the "absence of conversations in their homes about the professional or corporate sector" (Hirudayaraj & McLean, 2017, p. 97). Growing up in households where families discuss careers, finances, and education is an advantage most first-generation graduates do not enjoy. Participants of Hirudayaraj and McLean's (2017) study stated they "had not been aware of the professional world and its expectations in their student years, and therefore, they did not see the need to prepare themselves for a career" (p. 97).

This chapter looks beyond the college experience of first-generation graduates and reveals strategies for mid-level career success. Interviewing, salary negotiations, and networking advice is available from many articles and textbooks. However, that guidance does not tap into the assets and nuances first-generation graduates bring to the employment process. Garrison and Gardner (2012) studied the personal assets of first-generation college students; in their research, they concluded:

> [F]irst-generation college students in this study have the following personal assets: proactivity, goal direction, optimism and reflexivity. There were thirteen [13] contributing strengths that supported the asset development: resourcefulness, strategic thinking, self-reliance, practical realism, flexibility, persistence, positivity, hopefulness, self-confidence, insightfulness, compassion, gratitude, and balance. The development of the students' assets was influenced by their lived experience and occurred in response to their marginalized socio-cultural positioning. (p. 2)

Such skills are valuable in mid-level career development. They are essential to negotiating complex decisions and making life transitions. First-generation graduates have experience solving problems and taking steps to move forward, at times without the benefit of all the information. These skills inform how graduates navigate life transitions; they reveal how they balance strengths with challenges to initiate action.

Although first-generation graduates face some educational and early-career challenges, these challenges are not insurmountable. Because of their resilience, many first-generation graduates—such as Sonia Sotomayor, Associate Justice of the Supreme Court; Michelle Obama, 44th First Lady of the United States; Howard Schultz, Chairman and CEO of Starbucks; Colin Powell, former Secretary of State of the United States; Oprah Winfrey, television executive and media mogul; and Ruth Simmons, 18th president of Brown University—have gone on to make significant contributions to society.

First-generation Graduates at Mid-Level Career Growth

By midcareer, most early-career mistakes transform into life lessons. Accepting underemployment, failing to negotiate a salary, or missing out on professional networking are common mistakes made early in one's career. Mid-level career professionals must learn from these mistakes and use them for career opportunities in the future. First-generation graduates in mid-level careers should apply their lived experiences and transferable skills to excel in the search process (interviewing); forge professional networks; establish a personal brand; develop careers, not jobs; and accelerate financial planning.

Interviewing

Interviewing is anxiety-producing for most people. Thinking about how to prepare, dress, and what to ask is nerve-racking. Conventional advice minimizes good interviewing down to a firm handshake, eye contact, and professional attire—all important, but only a fraction of what is needed. At mid-career, first-generation graduates have advantages that set them apart.

- **Tell your story.** Being the first person in your family to earn a postsecondary degree is a significant accomplishment. It is connected to a story of sacrifice, achievement, and resilience. First-generation graduates overcame unique circumstances to achieve their goals. Their stories are a source of inspiration and a testament to character and work ethic. U.S. Supreme Court Justice Sonia Sotomayor was born in The Bronx, New York, to immigrant parents who spoke minimal English. Her father died when she was 9-years-old, and for most of her life, she was raised by a single parent. Sotomayor graduated summa cum laude from Princeton University and earned her Juris Doctorate from Yale Law School. Her story is unique and says even more about her qualifications. Find an opening in the conversation to share your story.

- **Take time to reflect.** Think back on your early career and look for lessons only seen in hindsight. Mistakes made, lessons learned, success stories, and failures are all valuable experiences. These experiences make you who you are. Throughout Oprah Winfrey's career, she capitalized on speaking her truth. Her brand is about being her authentic self. She works in a profession that pushes and pulls celebrities in every direction, but she remains grounded by continually reflecting on her true north. Mid-level careers come with more compensation, responsibility, and stress; staying grounded and speaking your truth is valuable. Reflect on life's lessons, mine them for strategies, and understand how they shaped your character and professional competence. Finding your authentic self requires reflection.

- **Proper preparation.** Take every interview opportunity seriously and prepare like a professional. Do your homework, read everything possible, and practice responses to as many interview questions as possible. Overprepare, practice every likely scenario, and know as much as possible about the institution and interviewers. Build a binder that includes the position description, your résumé, organizational charts, financial information, interview questions and answers, profiles of search committee members, and newspaper articles. Block out time on your schedule to study and absorb the information. These are skills many first-generation professionals mastered to graduate from college and gain success early in their careers— keep doing these things.

- **Work with search firms.** Search firms are one of the most critical tools mid-level career professionals have to maximize workforce opportunities. At this level, search firms coordinate hiring opportunities. Although these firms work on behalf of the employer, building relationships with them is invaluable. Search firm consultants attend professional conferences; they want to meet high-potential candidates and build their client base. Be intentional about getting to know consultants who work for higher education search firms. Contact a consultant before a conference, invite them to have a cup of coffee, share a copy of your résumé, and stay in touch. Your name in their database and a personal connection increases your chances of being invited into a search process. Even if you do not end up as the lead candidate, a rigorous search process is worth going through. If you are not a successful candidate, ask the search consultant for feedback. The key is building a relationship with a search firm.

Professional Networks

First-generation graduates at midcareer must develop their professional networks (Chapter 6 includes a more detailed networking discussion). Networking is a skill some develop naturally, while others might need coaching. Gibson et al. (2014) developed an integrated definition of networking, stating "networking is a form of goal-directed behavior, both inside and outside of an organization, focused on creating, cultivating, and utilizing interpersonal relationships" (p. 150). Networking behaviors include building, maintaining, and using internal and external networks (Wolff & Moser, 2009); socializing; engaging in professional activities, community activities, and internal visibility (Forret & Dougherty, 2004); as well as calling and visiting people, attending social activities, entertaining visitors, doing favors, providing mentoring, giving gifts, and forming alliances (Michael & Yukl, 1993). Researchers found it was essential to distinguish between internal networking with members of your organization versus external networking with people outside the organization, both are important but require different skill sets.

Professional networks develop over time, not overnight. Building mutually beneficial relationships, rather than transactional relationships, takes time. Networking relationships that focus on self-service are unlikely to mature to their full potential. Because networking happens over the long term, it may take months or years for benefits to materialize. When networking remains transactional, it fails to live up to its full potential; networking benefits depend on mutual support. In their research on internal and external networks, Michael and Yukl (1993) described networking as "calling and visiting people, socializing before and after regular formal meetings, attending social activities such as parties or lunches, conducting tours and entertaining visitors, doing favors, providing mentoring and advice, giving gifts, using forms of ingratiation such as praise and congratulations, forming alliances and sponsorships, passing on gossip and information that is important to another manager, and engaging in informal conversations about no work topics such as sports, family, and recreational activities" (p. 329). The distinction between internal and external networking is pertinent because strategies for success vary in each setting. To build external networks, mid-level career professionals should identify the value they bring to a relationship, whereas internal networks depend on organizational structure and access to resources.

A few developments in professional networking include the following:

- **A shift to individual responsibility.** Mid-level professionals often depend on employers to make meaningful career connections and finance their professional development; employers are shifting away from this. Researchers acknowledged a "shift" in employer-based networking behavior. Responsibility for networking behavior moved from the employer to the employee. Career management behaviors— networking, visibility, and self-development—belong to individual employees rather than employers (Wolff et al., 2018, p. 1). Forret and Dougherty (2004) concurred that "networking as a career management strategy is important, as the burden of responsibility for one's career has shifted from the organization to the individual" (p. 420). Building and maintaining a network has become an individual responsibility, not an employer's responsibility.

- **Network intensity, diversity, and quality matter.** Lambert et al. (2006) made distinctions between network intensity, diversity, and quality. They described network intensity as the amount of effort invested in building a professional network (intensity). Simultaneously, the type of contacts and value of information received from those contacts is its quality. The quality of networking is more important than the intensity or quantity of one's network. They also caution that when networks lack diversity (e.g., gender, race, age, region), this is negatively associated with the quality of information (p. 360). Mid-level professionals developing their career networks should focus on building and maintaining high-quality and diverse professional networks rather than a narrowly focused network of close friends. Meet new people, introduce them to your network, ask to be introduced to their network, stay in touch, and do your part to maintain the relationship.
- **Networking outcomes differ for men and women.** One might assume networking trends are the same for men and women; that assumption is false. Researchers found networking produced variable results for men versus women. Although there was "no difference in network diversity of information quality for gender or race, and no gender differences were found for network intensity" (Lambert et al., 2006, p. 361), women receive fewer career benefits than men for similar networking behaviors (Forret & Dougherty, 2004). Internal networking

activities led to increased compensation and promotions for men, but the same networking behaviors and internal visibility did not produce more compensation or promotions for women. All genders should be aware of this observation to neutralize this bias.

Do not take this aspect of mid-level career development for granted. Networking is perhaps the most crucial skill professionals must develop for sustainable career growth. It is our networks and experiences, not formal education, that help advance our careers. Professional networks require ongoing maintenance.

Personal Branding

Everyone has a personal brand—from multimillion-dollar companies to small businesses and individuals, everyone has a brand that needs development and protection. Mid-level career professionals must build their brand. Most understand the importance of protecting corporate brands like Walmart, Mercedes, Apple, Coca-Cola, and McDonald's. For example, in 2005, the United States District Court of the District of Oregon ruled in favor of Starbucks Corporation against Samantha Lundberg (*Starbucks Corp. v. Lundberg,* 2005).

Starbucks corporation brought a trademark infringement suit against Samantha Lundberg to use "Sambucks" as her coffee shop's name. Starbucks is a multimillion-dollar global company founded in 1971. At the time of the case, the company generated several billion dollars in revenue from locations across the United States and more than 30 countries. Samantha Lundberg owned a small coffee shop that posed no real threat to Starbucks's profitability, reputation, or brand; Starbucks thought otherwise. That year, Starbucks spent more than $200 million on advertising, promotion, and related marketing activities—television ads, radio commercials, print advertising, in-store displays, and product placement ads in motion pictures and television shows. In court, they argued, "Starbucks considers maintenance of its premium image to be particularly important;" therefore, "any use of variations on the Starbucks® mark on products that are not of the same premium reputation as Starbucks' products could decrease Starbucks' reputation" (p. 8). Starbucks argued that "Sambucks" could dilute the Starbucks brand by creating confusion ("blurring") in consumers' minds or creating an association ("tarnishment") in the minds of consumers that is inconsistent with the brand. The court ruled in favor of Starbucks and prohibited Samantha Lundberg from using the name "Sambucks" on her coffee shop.

Your reputation (or personal brand) is your most valuable asset. A poor reputation (e.g., lazy, does not follow through, does not get along with others, resistant to change) follows you throughout your career. Your coworkers are aware of your brand, and your future employers will be as well. Your social media profile is a projection of your brand. Protect your brand as fiercely as Starbucks protects theirs.

Your brand is integral to who you are—your social media profile, work performance, attitude, effort, follow-through, professional dress, listening skills, and communication skills. Do not be described by colleagues as lazy, late, chauvinistic, unreliable, manipulative, selfish, inconsiderate, or bossy. Your brand should be hardworking, dependable, consistent, and considerate. Everyone has a personal brand that requires maintenance. Part of your brand lives in a blind spot—behaviors observable to others but unknown to ourselves. Your reputation at work is a key factor in mid-level career success.

Strategies for building a professional brand include the following:

- **Follow through.** Do what you say you will do. A critical aspect of a personal brand is whether others can count on you to follow through. In some cases, a single inconsistency can result in missing out on an opportunity. Imagine, every work assignment is an interview. Build a reputation where people know they can count on you. Otherwise, consistent failure to follow through will become a permanent mark on your brand.

- **Show up on time.** Everyone is aware of that colleague who consistently shows up late to meetings. Showing up late, even by a few minutes, is noticeable and damaging to a professional reputation. At first, people ignore the minor disruption, but continued tardiness is distracting and noticeable. Consistent tardiness is a reflection of organizational skills and reliability. Everyone's time is valuable; showing up late communicates to others how little you value their time. Instead, arrive early to every meeting, and use that time to network with others who also show up early.
- **Dress for success.** Dress in a manner appropriate for the position you want next, not the job you have now. This advice is not exclusive to the interview process; this is good advice for day-to-day work. Professional dress is part of your brand. Although it is tempting to dress down (e.g., collared shirt and jeans) to match others, be mindful of how you show up every day and where you want to go. Even when the work environment encourages a casual dress code, consider your professional goals and take cues from your desired future.

Career Development

Maintain a commitment to professional growth. Working hard, showing up every day, and allowing a career to evolve organically is one approach. This approach is the most common and least stressful, but the problem is that it leaves your career development in others' hands. An alternative path involves leveraging your current role to develop skills and capacity for future opportunities. Limited funding for professional development opportunities off-campus should not be a concern; there are countless opportunities to grow professional skills in on-campus projects. Turn every role and project into a professional development opportunity. Commit to ongoing education—both formal (e.g., certificate or degree programs) and informal (e.g., committees, task forces, projects). Invest the time and effort to build subject matter expertise on at least one challenge per year; this will exceed what you would have learned attending a conference presentation.

Serve on committees and task force assignments related to important university decisions; make tangible contributions to the project and outcomes. Shadow a senior executive who oversees units about which you want to learn more. Seek mentors on campus that can provide periodic advice. Read and write about the profession and make contributions to the literature via conference presentations and publications. Take risks that put you outside of your comfort zone. A well-planned career involves calculated risk-taking (e.g., accepting a new position, requesting a promotion, switching careers, starting a business, writing a book, earning a degree in an unrelated field). Many mid-level professionals are hesitant to take risks because there is often a lot to lose, yet risk-taking is an essential career advancement step.

Financial Planning

Mid-level career professionals often overlook financial planning. Many are approaching their peak earning years, and poor financial planning could derail life goals and retirement. Financial planning is vital on the job as well as in life. Chapter 4 includes a more thorough discussion on financial literacy.

First-generation professions are particularly vulnerable to financial mistakes because of lingering student debt and lack of mentors. In 2018, the Federal Reserve reported student loan debt exceeded $1.5 trillion, surpassing almost every kind of debt, including credit card debt

(Board of Governors of the Federal Reserve, 2018). The same report revealed first-generation graduates were "more likely to be behind on their payments than those with a parent who completed college" (Board of Governors of the Federal Reserve, 2018, para. 11). Table 8.1 illustrates where parents of college graduates have at least a bachelor's degree, only 5 percent of their students were behind on student loan payments. On the other hand, where parents do not have a college degree (first-generation students), 14 percent of their students were behind on student loan payments. Parents' education makes a difference in whether their graduate is behind on their student loans.

Table 8.1

Payment Status of Loans for Own Education, by Parents' Education

Status	Not first-generation college students (all)	First-generation college students (all)
Behind	5%	14%
Current	47%	39%
Paid off	47%	47%

Note. From *Report on the Economic Well-Being of U.S. Households in 2017–May 2018,* by Board of Governors of the Federal Reserve System, 2018 (https://www.federalreserve. gov/publications/2018-economic-well-being-of-us-households-in-2017-student-loans. htm#xfigure32-paymentstatusofloansforown-876ab9ec). In the public domain.

Debt influences mid-level career decision making. In the early stages of one's career, debt influences the type of risks and opportunities that first-generation graduates consider. According to the Federal Reserve 2018 report, 22 percent of first-generation graduates are behind on their student loan payments, compared to only 5 percent for graduates who are not first-generation. Personal finances influence early and mid-level career choices. Opportunites that debt-free graduates consider (e.g., foreign exchange experiences, sabbaticals, post-doctoral research) are often out of range for mid-level career professionals who are balancing debt.

Table 8.2

Payment Status of Loans for Own Education, by Graduates' Age

Status	Not first-generation college students (ages 18–29)	First-generation college students (ages 18–29)
Behind	5%	22%
Current	72%	64%
Paid off	23%	14%

Note. From *Report on the Economic Well-Being of U.S. Households in 2017–May 2018,* by Board of Governors of the Federal Reserve System, 2018 (https://www.federalreserve. gov/publications/2018-economic-well-being-of-us-households-in-2017-student-loans. htm#xfigure32-paymentstatusofloansforown-876ab9ec). In the public domain.

Financial independence—that is, freedom to make career and life decisions on your terms—is often considered impossible by some educational professionals. This mindset is ingrained into the professional's psyche and inhibits personal sacrifices that would lead to financial independence. In truth, financial independence is accessible through a disciplined approach to (1) eliminating debt, (2) building savings, and (3) personal investing.

1. **Eliminate debt.** Financial independence is not possible as long as you are paying a debt. In his best-selling book *Financial Peace Revisited*, Dave Ramsey (2002) introduced seven steps to financial freedom. In the first two steps, he suggested establishing an emergency fund and paying off debt. Even high-wage earners will not achieve financial independence if consumed by debt (e.g., car payments, student loans, credit cards). A considerable portion of household incomes is committed to paying interest-bearing debts. Financial advisors suggest several debt elimination strategies; the bottom line is to have a debt elimination plan and commit to it. Getting rid of debt is the first step in gaining financial independence. The next steps—saving and investing—can not be maximized as long as debt remains.

2. **Build savings.** The U.S. Bureau of Economic Analysis (2021) reported the monthly personal savings rate from 2015–2020 was 13.7 percent. The personal savings rate is the ratio of personal savings compared to disposable income. U.S. consumers spent more than 86 percent of their monthly income, most of which on debt. As a result, most Americans hold minimal savings in their account. They deposit their paycheck, pay debts, and then spend the remainder on leisure activities. Whatever is deposited in savings is usually consumed before the end of each month. Building financial independence requires disciplined spending and saving.

   Within a budget, set a target to save a larger and larger percentage of your monthly income. Pay your savings account as if it were a bill, then pay your bills. Identify and eliminate nonessential expenses, such as that gym membership you rarely use and subscription services you do not need. Plan and prepare meals at home rather than eating out. Reduce required expenses (e.g., gas, electricity, water, food) as much as possible. Transfer those unspent dollars into a savings account and leave them there. With your bank, set up a process to automatically deposit an amount of money from your paycheck into savings. Do not trust yourself to make this transaction every pay period—make it happen automatically. If you live in a household with two incomes, reduce expenses to the point where a single income can cover all expenses; the second income is devoted entirely to savings and investing. Saving cannot be accomplished without eliminating debt. With a comfortable savings account (6 to 9 months of expenses), shift your attention to investing.

3. **Invest.** You and your employer invest in your retirement through a defined contribution program—TIAA CREF or Vanguard. This money is not accessible to you, without steep penalties, until retirement age. Mid-level professionals should

know how their retirement is invested—low risk, moderate risk, or high risk. Have a conversation with your retirement investment representative, ask questions, check the account's balance, maximize your contribution, and discuss how much is needed to achieve your retirement goals.

Aside from your employer-based retirement account, invest on your own. A Gallup poll found that only 52 percent of Americans invested in the stock market in 2016 (McCarthy, 2016), the lowest investment rate in nearly 20 years. Most Americans avoid investing in the stock market because they believe they do not earn enough or know enough about the market. For entry-level investors, investing has become much easier through do-it-yourself platforms designed for low-budget, nonprofessional investors.

There is a difference between investing, speculating, and day trading. *Investing* is a long-term strategy, making regular deposits in a balanced portfolio of stocks and exchange-traded funds. Investors are not distracted by start-up ventures or market fluctuations; they invest for the long term. *Speculating*, however, involves investing in high-risk opportunities in hopes of a large profit over a short period, such as flipping real estate, investing in initial public offerings (IPOs), or "get rich quick" schemes. Alternately, *day trading* involves attempts to outsmart the market by buying and selling stocks every day. Speculating and day trading are high risks and require a significant amount of time and attention.

On the other hand, investing entails getting to know companies with a track record of positive returns and making consistent investments over time. Funds invested are accessible at all times, but withdrawals can be taxed based on capital gains. The advantage to investing is compound interest; while savings accounts lose value over time due to inflation, investments gain value due to compound interest. Commit to a monthly investment amount. Small investments grow into large sums over time. It's never too late to start.

Conclusion

The purpose of this chapter was to examine the advantages first-generation graduates have in mid-level careers. By overcoming educational challenges and early-career obstacles, first-generation graduates at midcareer have a wealth of experiences to draw from that make them uniquely qualified for success—that is, only if they take advantage of those opportunities. They must leverage those experiences into tangible assets during the interview process, build professional networks, establish and protect their brand, and accelerate financial planning. First-generation graduates have compelling stories of resilience and perseverance that set them apart. They must invest in building robust and diverse professional networks that pay dividends throughout their careers. Understanding that everyone has a personal brand is a considerable hurdle; their non-first-generation peers who bypass them in early-career opportunities may come from households where personal branding and professional networks were developed via their parents or siblings. Getting comfortable with the idea that career development happens every day *on the job* is essential; waiting for career development to come from outside experiences is wasting valuable time and energy. The mid-level is also a critical stage to begin looking at long-term financial planning: debt reduction, saving, and investing. Simply put, the more professionals focus on their finances at this stage, the better positioned they will be to make career choices and take risks.

Questions for Reflection

1. What is your story? Your life has been full of experiences that have shaped you in ways you have not yet realized. Reflect on your story, and do not be afraid to share it as a testimony of your character.

2. Start your professional network today. Think about three to five internal and external relationships you intend to build in the next 12 months. Be specific. Be intentional. Be proactive.

3. You have a personal brand worthy of development and protection. Think about how you have displayed your brand thus far. Would others describe you as hardworking, disciplined, dependable, and collaborative? Or might they say you are untrustworthy, unreliable, inconsistent, and self-aggrandizing? It takes courage to find these things out about yourself, yet reshaping your brand is within your direct control. Start now.

4. In what ways have you left your career to chance, to the whims of others? Do you live under constant anxiety that you are not in control of your career destiny? If you answered yes to either question, get intentional about your career path—right now.

5. Are you prepared financially to make decisions that serve your interest? Most mid- and senior-level career professionals are not. Personal Finance 101: pay off debt, save, and invest. We think careers in education do not allow for financial independence, but that's not true. With careful planning, mid-level professionals can build strong financial portfolios.

References

Board of Governors of the Federal Reserve System. (2018). *Report on the economic well-being of U.S. households in 2017–May 2018.* https://www.federalreserve.gov/publications/2018-economic-well-being-of-us-households-in-2017-student-loans.htm#xfigure32-paymentstatusofloansforown-876ab9ec

Choy, S. P. (2001). *Students whose parents did not go to college: Postsecondary access, persistence, and attainment: NCES 2001–126.* U.S. Department of Education, National Center for Education Statistics. https://nces.ed.gov/pubs2001/2001126.pdf

Chen, X., & Carroll, C. D. (2005). *First-generation students in postsecondary education: A look at their college transcripts* (NCES 2005-171). U.S. Department of Education, National Center for Education Statistics. https://nces.ed.gov/pubs2005/2005171.pdf

Collier, P. J., & Morgan, D. L. (2008). "Is that paper really due today?": Differences in first-generation and traditional college students' understandings of faculty expectations. *Higher Education, 55*(4), 425–446. https://doi.org/10.1007/s10734-007-9065-5

Forret, M. L., & Dougherty, T. W. (2004). Networking behaviors and career outcomes: Differences for men and women? *Journal of Organizational Behavior, 25*, 283–311. https://doi.org/10.1002/job.253

Garrison, N. J., & Gardner, D. S. (2012, November 15–18). *Assets first-generation college students bring to the higher education setting* [Paper presentation]. Association for the Study of Higher Education 37th Annual Conference, Las Vegas, NV, United States.

Gibson, C., Hardy, J. H., & Buckley, M. R. (2014). Understanding the role of networking in organizations. *Career Development International, 19*(2), 146–161. https://doi.org/10.1108/CDI-09-2013-0111

Hirudayaraj, M., & McLean, G. N. (2017). First-generation college graduates: A phenomenological exploration of their transition experiences into the corporate sector. *European Journal of Training and Development, 42*(1/2), 91–109. https://doi.org/10.1108/EJTD-06-2017-0055

Horn, L., & Nunez, A. M. (2000). *Mapping the road to college: First-generation students' math track, planning strategies, and context of support: NCES 2000–153.* U.S. Department of Education, National Center for Education Statistics.

Jehangir, R. R. (2009). Cultivating voices: First-generation students seek full academic citizenship in multicultural learning communities. *Innovative Higher Education, 34*(1), 33–49. https://doi.org/10.1007/s10755-008-9089-5

Kabaci, M. J., & Cude, B. J. (2015). A delphi study to identify personal finance core concepts and competencies of first-generation college students. *Family and Consumer Sciences Research Journal, 43*(3), 244–258.

Lambert, T. A., Eby, L. T., & Reeves, M. P. (2006). Predictors of networking intensity and network quality among white-collar job seekers. *Journal of Career Development, 32*(4), 351–365. https://doi.org/10.1177%2F0894845305282767

Lohfink, M. M., & Paulsen, M. B. (2005). Comparing the determinants of persistence for first-generation and continuing-generation students. *Journal of College Student Development, 46*(4), 409–428. https://doi.org/10.1353/csd.2005.0040

McCarthy, J. (2016). Just over half of Americans own stocks, matching record lows. *Gallup News*. https://news.gallup.com/poll/190883/half-americans-own-stocks-matching-record-low.aspx

Michael, J., & Yukl, G. (1993). Managerial level and submit function as determinants of networking behavior in organizations. *Group and Organization Management*, *18*(3), 328–351. https://doi.org/10.1177%2F1059601193183005

Ramsey, D. (2002). *Financial peace revisited: New chapters on marriage, singles, kids and families.* Viking Books.

Starbucks Corp. v. Lundberg, 2005 U.S. Dist. Lexis 32660 (D. Or. 2005).

Stieha, V. (2010). Expectations and experiences: The voice of a first-generation first-year college student and the question of student persistence. *International Journal of Qualitative Studies in Education*, *23*(2), 237–249. https://doi.org/10.1080/09518390903362342

Thayer, P. B. (2000, May). Retention of students from first-generation and low-income backgrounds *Opportunity Outlook*, 2–8. https://files.eric.ed.gov/fulltext/ED446633.pdf

U.S. Bureau of Economic Analysis. (2021). *Personal saving rate [PSAVERT]*. https://fred.stlouisfed.org/series/PSAVERT

Wolff, H.-G., & Moser, K. (2009). Effects of networking on career success: A longitudinal study. *Journal of Applied Psychology*, *94*(1), 196–206. https://doi.org/10.1037/a0013350

Wolff, H.-G., Weikamp, J. G., & Batinic, B. (2018). Implicit motives as determinants of networking behaviors. *Frontiers in Psychology*, *9*, Article 411. https://doi.org/10.3389/fpsyg.2018.00411

9

How Being a First-generation Graduate Influences Faculty Experiences

Sonja Ardoin, Claudia García-Louis, and Darris R. Means

In the past decade, researchers and scholars have increasingly examined the educational experiences, opportunities, and challenges of first-generation college students in undergraduate and graduate programs (see, e.g., Ardoin, 2018; Gardner & Holley, 2011; Holley & Gardner, 2012; Padgett et al., 2012; Soria & Stebleton, 2012; Toutkoushian et al., 2018; Vuong et al., 2010). As first-generation college students ourselves, we recognize the importance of this scholarship and research for promoting equity and justice for these students. At the same time, our identity as first-generation college students did not end at the conclusion of our doctoral programs. In fact, we continue to navigate the unspoken rules of academia, negotiating our experiences, hopes, and challenges as faculty members. Furthermore, we recognize that our existence within academe cannot be understood in isolation; our status as first-generation faculty members should be considered at the intersection of other identities (e.g., race, ethnicity, gender, class, sexuality, caregiver status, nation of origin).

In this chapter, we begin with an overview of positions and pathways of the professoriate. We then share our individual stories of how being a first-generation faculty member influences our teaching, research, service, pedagogy, and philosophies. Scholars have discussed the power of storytelling as a way to center the experiences of people within their marginalized identities and to challenge deficit-oriented narratives embedded in racism, classism, and other forms of oppression (Delgado, 1989; Pérez Huber & Cueva, 2016). Recognizing the intersection of our multiple social identities, Sonja and Darris present their experiences and stories as first-generation faculty members as narratives, and Claudia presents her story through the use of *testimonio*, a method for reassigning "agency to Chicana/Latina scholars through the telling of one's history as part of a larger collective memory" (Pérez Huber & Cueva, 2016, p. 35). After sharing our individual narratives and *testimonio,* we examine similarities, differences, and connections across our stories. We end with reflection questions and suggested exercises educators can utilize to center the voices of first-generation college students.

Positions and Pathways of the Professoriate

Teacher. Educator. Researcher. Scholar. Advisor. Mentor. Faculty member. These are just some of the many terms used to describe individuals who are tasked with cultivating the academic mission of colleges and universities. Much like these multiple descriptors, there are numerous ways to pursue the professoriate, including different types of positions with unique combinations of teaching, research, and service responsibilities within particular institutional contexts. As first-generation college students navigate the higher education environment and possibly consider pursuing faculty life, it can be helpful for them to understand the different positions within and pathways to the professoriate.

Faculty members can be hired for part-time (e.g., adjunct) or full-time capacities. They can fill roles that are considered contingent with fixed-term or renewable contracts or tenure-track roles with an initial 6-year probationary period before a peer vote to determine if the individual secures permanent employment (Shelton & Ardoin, 2020). Each of these tracks comes with different "ranks" or title codes, such as instructor and lecturer ranks, clinical or teaching ranks, and tenure-track ranks. Instructor and lecturer ranks often have two levels: instructor/lecturer and senior instructor/lecturer. Clinical or teaching ranks typically offer three levels: clinical assistant professor, clinical associate professor, and professor of the practice. Tenure-track ranks are also structured into three levels: assistant professor, associate professor, and full professor. Although many faculty members are called *professor* by students, the term is truly accurate for only a small percentage, because approximately 43% of faculty are in part-time roles and another 20% are in full-time, non-tenure-track lines (Haviland et al., 2017). This means contingent faculty compose almost two thirds of the overall faculty workforce (Shelton & Ardoin, 2020).

There is no fixed definition or workload for faculty members across academic disciplines and institutional types. Every faculty member will engage in some combination of teaching, research, and service; however, their responsibilities may focus more heavily on one particular element of the "academic trifecta" depending on the type of institution where they work. For example, community colleges and regional public institutions frequently require faculty to be focused teachers who are skilled at pedagogical innovation and active advising processes, and research-focused institutions may put more emphasis on their faculty members' ability to publish peer-reviewed research and achieve national prominence in their respective fields.

This does not mean the former group of faculty do not engage in research or scholarly activities, nor does it mean the latter group are not quality course instructors. Rather, it means that "productivity" is assessed differently based on institutional type.

People often find their way to the professoriate through graduate-level study. They may be invited to co-teach a course as a teaching assistant or coauthor papers as a research assistant, and they enjoy one or both of those processes enough to consider embracing this career pathway. However, other individuals arrive to the academy from their roles in industry (e.g., business, communications, photography, technology), bridging theory to practice in the classroom as *scholar–practitioners* of their fields of choice. Thus, some faculty members have followed what is considered "traditional" trajectories to the professoriate: undergraduate degree, graduate degree(s), post-doctoral research role, then full-time faculty position. Others have charted their own maps to academia: for example, undergraduate degree, full-time job(s), completing a graduate degree part time while working, guest lecturer, then part-time or adjunct instructor while maintaining their industry role. The point is, there are multiple ways to get to the professoriate and shape students' higher education learning environments.

Although each of the chapter authors' pathways to the professoriate were very distinct, our experiences as first-generation college students meant we encountered similar obstacles, and all three of us began our careers as student affairs educators and later shifted to faculty roles. Sonja's faculty career began as student affairs educator, as a part-time, adjunct instructor of first-year experience and leadership courses. Then, 3 years after earning her PhD, she became a full-time, non-tenure-track clinical assistant professor. She now serves in a tenure-track assistant professor post. Claudia decided to attend graduate school after directing an office of multicultural affairs for 3 years; her original goal was to become a vice provost of student affairs. However, after getting involved in a research team during her PhD program, she decided to pursue the professoriate. Upon graduation she served as a visiting professor for a year before accepting a tenure-track faculty position. Darris worked full time during his entire PhD program, so he transitioned from a full-time staff member to a tenure-track assistant professor upon graduation. He was promoted to a tenured, associate professor during his sixth year at his current university.

In the following section, through Sonja's and Darris' narratives and Claudia's *testimonio,* we describe how we have navigated and experienced being first-generation college graduates and, now, faculty members. Furthermore, we explain how the layering of other identities (e.g., race, ethnicity, gender, class, sexuality, caregiver status, nation of origin) with first-generation college graduate status influences our teaching, research, service, and pedagogical practices. We wrote our narratives/*testimonio* in isolation before we convened to discuss the chapter. We wanted to ensure each of us reflected (in our own way) what influences, motivates, and encourages us to be faculty members. After our narratives/*testimonio* we interrogate commonalities and differences among our reflections.

The Hustle for a "Better Life": Sonja's Narrative as a First-generation Faculty Member

I grew up in a small, rural community in south central Louisiana in a working-class family that believed education was a pathway to a "better life," though no one explained what that meant or why I should pursue this pathway that had not been available to anyone in my family or many in our community. I was taught to love books at an early age by my maternal grandmother, my MawMaw, who saw to it that I was a frequent patron of the local library. My reading habits were affirmed by my parents, who obliged my requests for books as gifts.

This fascination with books and reading translated into my passion for school. As a child I would line up stuffed animals or dolls and "teach" to them. I loved the learning process, though I would not have called it that then. The teachers at my small, local, rural public K–12 school nurtured my curiosity (likely because I had the privileges of being White and able). My maternal grandfather, my PawPaw, rewarded me with $5 for all As on a report card. Consequently, I learned early on that education was tied to money and that, if I wanted the "better life" people hoped and prayed I could get, I would have to figure out how to get the money that I would need to seek more education. These elements of my childhood—combined with my marginalized identities of being a woman in a working-class, rural community and my privileged identities of being White, straight, and able—are probably how I developed my proclivity to perceive educational productivity as a hustle and, sometimes, a fulfilling endeavor.

So, I hustled. I got the As (and the $5 bills). I played every sport my school offered. I joined 4-H, Future Farmers of America, Future Business Leaders of America, student council, and French club. I learned the details of Louisiana's merit-based tuition opportunity program so I knew what courses I had to take, what grade point average I had to earn, and what standardized test scores I needed to hit, and I set out to do the damn thing. That hustle earned me a spot at what I considered the best public university in the state, our flagship—Louisiana State University—and I got to live out my family's collective dream of pursuing higher education, as the inaugural member of my family to do so. I will never forget opening my acceptance letter, thinking, "This changes everything," and feeling simultaneously thrilled and terrified about what that might mean.

Lessons Learned as a First-generation College Student

Being a first-generation student taught me the value of knowing and appreciating where I come from, persisting, becoming comfortable with risk taking, asking questions, finding community, and pursuing my own pathway. I learned that my roots were assets; I knew how to work hard, be creative, and appreciate simplicity, all of which served me well as someone who majored in education three times (i.e., bachelor's, master's, and PhD). I knew the chips would not always fall my way and that I had to persevere. So, when I got a less-than-stellar grade or got rejected from something to which I applied, I took a moment to mourn then got back to business. I was aware that there was a lot I did not know or understand, so I became comfortable with taking risks and asking questions. I recognized the significance of community and sought it in new spaces, often finding it in those who shared similar roots, such as other first-generation college students or students from poor or working-class backgrounds. I understood that I was on a trajectory that no one in my family had experienced or could demystify for me. I had to pursue my own pathway and lean on my newly developed community, inviting advice and direction from peers and mentors and then deciding what made sense for me. I also continued to hustle as an undergraduate, master's, and PhD student. I applied for every scholarship for which I qualified, I joined (too many) organizations, and I still strove for all As, though the $5 payout shifted to the emotional payoff of seeing my PawPaw hold my diplomas in his hands in sheer wonder and pride.

Being a First-generation College Student and Faculty Member

Because of my experiences as first-generation student and graduate, as a faculty member I both accept and reject that educational productivity is a hustle, and I maintain that it can and should be a fulfilling endeavor. I accept the hustle in that I feel a persistent and pervasive need to prove my worth, my belonging, my place; to work harder and produce more; to make sure all my proverbial ducks are in a row so that I do not get "found out" (see Chapter 2 for more on imposter syndrome). I position myself in ways that prepare me for future opportunities, though I am not always sure what those are or if I even want them. I believe faculty life makes many people feel this way; however, I would argue the pressure to hustle is heightened for first-generation college graduates and individuals with minoritized identities and is even further elevated in institutions that feed off elitism and perpetuate identity-based "-isms." I have experienced the -isms of academia in comments such as a tenured White male professor chiding me for being "the little girl who doesn't know how to do anything around here" as a first semester doctoral student, and a White male associate dean invalidating all of my educational and professional experiences when frankly informing me that "no one at the [private] university cares what public schools do." It is moments like these that drive me to reject educational productivity as a hustle, because even 20 years of hustle cannot outweigh systemic bias and oppression.

As such, I also utilize my role as a faculty member to push against the system when it is compromising people's humanity, inhibiting people's access or denying their contributions, or upholding oppressive systems. I attempt to reject the hustle of conforming to the status quo (e.g., educational productivity, -isms) in favor of creating more equity through both individual choices and collaborative efforts. From the individual frame, I stand firm in using transparent language in my research and writing on social class and classism. Although reviewers call my use of terms such as *poor* and *working class* uncouth or extreme, I believe in questioning who gets to decide what language is "appropriate" and in reclaiming these terms. I also elect to contribute to organizations that are working to create access and equity and recognize individuals' humanity, such as the Center for First-generation Student Success, NASPA's Socioeconomic and Class Issues in Higher Education Knowledge Community, and the Social Justice Training Institute. Further, I attempt to disrupt the narrative that journal articles are the only valuable "currency" of the professoriate. I do not want to write only for other academics, so I focus on writing books and book chapters that I hope invite scholar-practitioners to focus on recognizing bias, inequity, and oppression and consider how educators might move forward to focus on people's humanity and assets as a means of fostering inclusion and equity. Although I have more leverage to make this kind of decision about my publishing practice as someone with multiple privileged identities, I recognize this choice might limit some future career possibilities, and thus my salary, and I have reconciled that the academy's definition of success is likely different from my own.

From the collaborative frame, as a faculty member I have the opportunity and responsibility to address access barriers for graduate student admissions and enrollment, such as the graduate record exam (GRE). If educators and institutions know the GRE is biased based on race, class, and gender, then why keep using it? When I arrived at my current institution, I lobbied my program faculty to remove the GRE from its admissions requirements in order to better live out the program values of inclusion and equity and the institutional value of inclusive excellence. Within a year, our program faculty were successful in making this shift and moving toward a more justice-based admissions practice. These are small, yet tangible, ways that I can contribute to rejecting the educational hustle—that productivity is prosperity and success can only be defined in narrow, quantifiable ways (e.g., grades, the number of journal article one publishes)—and reframing education as the opportunity for deliberate growth and discovering what success means for each individual.

Although some parts of academia will never make sense to me as a first-generation college graduate, I am affirmed by the fact that I get to live my passions—reading, learning, creating, and advocating—through my career. As a faculty member, I get to be a part of furthering representation for first-generation college students, individuals from rural areas, and people from poor and working-class backgrounds through my teaching, research, and service. I appreciate the privilege it is to live out the so-called "better life" on the shoulders of my giants—my grandparents, my parents, and my community—and to engage in work that, for the most part, feeds my soul.

Mi Existencia: Claudia's Testimonio

I find the process of writing about myself both daunting and liberating. This practice is very recent for me and began with my discovery of Chicana feminist epistemologies, ontologies, and methodologies. After reading the works of Dolores Delgado Bernal, Norma E. Cantú, Gloria Anzaldúa, and many other Chicana scholars, I was reminded that it was vital I love and embrace my *cultura*—my ancestry. The teachings of Anzaldúa (2012) continuously inspire me to bring my authentic self to all I do, even if it means being labeled as deficient by some. Chicana feminist traditions gave me permission to theorize and make sense of my experiences while celebrating my multiple marginalized identities. They provided a vital link between myself and academe—something I had not experienced in my more than 22 years of education. I finally see myself as capable of producing knowledge and *qualified* to make unique contributions to the field of education without the worry of "will I be perceived as competent enough?"

Given that *testimonio* disrupts the silence of those made mute by academia and humanizes their experiences while also validating their stories (Delgado Bernal, 2001; Delgado Bernal et al., 2016), I share my *testimonio* to make visible what many Latinx/a/o experience in academe. I write about navigating academe as a Mexican immigrant, the first in my family to graduate from high school, a first-generation college student, and now, a faculty member.

Infinite Possibilities?

I was born in Yahualica, Jalisco, Mexico, a small, quiet town known for making incredibly delicious hot sauce and not much else. At the age of 4, my family immigrated to the United States in search of a better future. I vividly remember speaking gibberish with my siblings as we pretended to be fluent in English, looking forward to someday being bilingual: being *American*. Although we were ecstatic about the infinite possibilities available to us via the American dream, we were oblivious to how hard we would have to work to keep our *cultural* identity intact. For me, public school was a place where I could no longer be Claudia García Medina. My teachers and school staff would butcher my name, they pronounced it Clawdea Garzah—removing the Medina from my name, effectively truncating my matrilineal connection. I quickly became acclimated to my educators not saying my name correctly, robbing me of my identity and labeling me a perpetual foreigner through my enforced enrollment in English language learner classes that did me no good as I was fluent in English. I became numb to the fact that the public school curriculum completely ignored my existence and fed me lies about Latinx/a/o students' inherent lack of academic potential.

Now, as a faculty member, I have the conceptual understanding to know that public school policies have long reinforced deculturaliza-tion—stripping non-White children of their culture and replacing it with that of the dominant group (Spring, 2016). For me, the result was devastating, as it unleashed a lifetime of insecurities related to being a Mexican immigrant in the United States; leaving me to con-stantly doubt my fit in academia. As a child, I was forced to assimilate because I wanted to belong. I began hiding my *tacos de frijoles*, *mangos con chile*, and *pepinos con sal y limón* that my *mamá* had carefully pre-pared for me. I wanted Lunchables, like all the other children were eating. I also began saying that I was born in Los Angeles—a small fib that I continued to recount through middle school—all in an effort to fit in, to assimilate.

Despite my desperate attempts to assimilate, I was seen as an outsider and was accepted only when I stopped speaking Spanish. Through all this, my parent's *consejos* continuously echoed in my head: *"Estudien para que no tengan que trabajar como burros como nosotros."* Their dream was to give us an equitable opportunity to receive an education, something that was not afforded to them. My father has a third-grade education and my mother completed only the sixth grade; their dream was for their children to at least finish high school. However, my two older siblings did not survive the effects of deculturalization imposed upon them by a subtractive public school education. My brother dropped out in middle school and my sister before completing high school. I was the first in my family to graduate from high school and go on to college. This was a huge accomplishment that came with added pressures and feelings of isolation. My parents were happy about my academic success but did not know how to support me. For example, when I would come home to share the new ideas I had learned, they seemed annoyed by my newfound identity and would often respond with, *"Aayyy si muy inteligente, te crees gringa."* I quickly discovered that being first in a family to graduate from high school and a first-generation college student could not be understood in isolation, as their intersection amounted to real-life material consequences for my entire family. To understand how I navigated and survived schooling, I needed to assess my P–20 educational experience in the context of my multiple marginalized identities, contemporary sociocultural factors, and family culture.

I Am My Father's Dream

As the survivor of a subtractive K–12 education and someone who "beat the odds" (emphasis on the quotation marks), I still very often feel inadequate in academic spaces despite being a faculty member. In reflecting on why this may be, I concluded it is a side effect of being forced to assimilate into a culture that could not (or would not) accept me as a first-generation Mexican immigrant. In fact, I have to actively work against lies my educators taught me about myself and my academic potential: No, I am not an affirmative action case. No, my culture is not deficient. No, being Mexican does not mean I am intellectually inferior. In retrospect, I realize my presence in college classrooms was more beneficial to affluent White students than it was for me. I taught them something they would have never learned through textbooks, as the stories of people like myself are often omitted from textbooks, and professors are often far disconnected from the realities of students who hold multiple marginalized identities. I did not realize it then—but I do now—that when I spoke about my experiences in the classroom, I was sharing my *testimonio*. I was attempting to find common ground with my classmates while (re)claiming my identity as an intellectual—a producer of knowledge. I was demanding my humanity that had been robbed by negative stereotypes and deficit assumptions about my people, about me, and my future.

I come from a people who tell stories that can be traced back for generations. Our stories have the remarkable power to document important pivotal moments that encapsulate the wisdom of our ancestors. Their wisdom is passed down from generation to generation, breathing air into tired bodies. Those stories are lifelines to our *antepasados* shared in the form of *enseñanzas*, *consejos*, and *regaños*. As I reflect on life-changing experiences that motivate me to work harder and assert my presence in academic spaces, there is one moment in my life that consistently rises to the top. When I was 5 years old, my father and I went to the grocery store. Out of nowhere an elderly White man began yelling at my father, "Go back to your country you F—-ing Mexican." To this day, I still cannot shake the look in my *papi*'s eyes. That verbal attack transmitted a clear message that not even children were safe from hate. I do not know how my father kept it together, but he did. I often share this story with my students because it underscores the importance of listening to one another; our stories make us who we are. What would have happened if the elderly man would have sat down with my father and heard his *testimonio*? How would he have reacted to my father's ethic of working from sunrise to sunset to earn a combined (his and my mother's) income of $19,000 a year? What would he say to their meticulous financial planning strategy of stretching that money enough to sustain a family of seven? My parents rejected the idea of applying for government assistance or any other type of social support. They wanted to prove they could do it on their own. Would he recognize that my parents made the difficult decision to move their entire family, away from loved ones, their culture, and language, for a possible (not even secured) better future? Could he have even begun to fathom how incredibly difficult that must have been?

I often tell my students that we see people, but we have no idea what stories they would tell. In this situation, the experience was terrible (and traumatizing), but the long-term consequences were not. My respect and admiration for my father have grown every day since that incident. I remember turning to him and whispering, "*Yo voy a estudiar por ti papi.*" He smiled at me, and we continued shopping. My personal experiences impact all aspects of my professional identity. How could they not? It is because of those experiences that I teach with compassion, love, and empathy. My personal struggles have forced me to see the humanity in all of us—we all carry and process our trauma differently.

An Inclusive Pedagogy

As a junior faculty member on the tenure track, I benefit from culturally inclusive academic spaces and critical scholarship just as much as my students. Therefore, my goal as an educator is to transform the classroom into a place where students' intellectual and theoretical curiosities are recognized and supported. I do not want them to experience the type of education I endured. For example, I did not read asset-based research about Latinx/a/o students until I found it for myself in my doctoral program. It has a profoundly negative impact on me and my intellectual curiosity. Now, as a faculty member, I make sure my students are exposed to the scholarship written by a variety of marginalized scholars, and I place them as seminal in all my courses. I also share my personal stories of navigating and surviving academia. I tell them that I chose to work at a Hispanic-serving institution because I know exactly what it feels like to be taught by a largely White faculty (I had a total of three Latinx/a/o professors in my entire education). It created a severe disconnect for me as I knew that regardless of how much they tried, they could never fully understand how academia for me was both a place of infinite possibilities and daily microaggressions. Thus, students are guaranteed to hear a bit of my *testimonio*; it is part of my pedagogical practice and a way to connect with them (García-Louis, 2019). It is my hope that through this practice they will be able to relate to their professor and to see the possibility of one day becoming a researcher or an educator. I want my students to know that, regardless of who they are and whatever their background may be, their educational experiences are just as important as the students sitting next to them.

In my teaching, I channel the spirit of Luis Valdez's (1994) use of Mayan precept—*In Lak'ech* which translates to *you are my other me*—to honor the contributions of my students just as much as I honor the works of other scholars. After all, my students' resilience, tenacity, and will to persist despite multiple obstacles should be celebrated. I thank them for their presence in the classroom and encourage them to share their *testimonios* whenever they feel fit. As a first-generation college graduate and now a faculty member, I consider how my personal and professional experiences, and the intersectionality of my identities, inform my pedagogical practice. In doing so, I am asserting my place in academic spaces, producing asset-based research about Latinx/a/o college students, and fulfilling the promise I once made to my *papi* of pursuing a college education. The college classroom provides a critical location from which to close the achievement gap—where an equitable learning environment has the power to foster the holistic development of students, so long as they are supported by inclusive pedagogies and epistemologies. It is because of my marginalized identities, not in spite of them, that I am able to motivate and support my students. The mutual exchange of *testimonios* simply humanizes the process.

Remembering My Roots: Darris' Narrative as a First-generation Faculty Member

"I want you to go to college." This was a constant statement from my mother during my childhood. My mother was a single parent who earned her high school diploma; she worked at a gas station to financially support our family, and we constantly discussed education as a family. The constant reminder about college became my initial drive for pursuing postsecondary education after my mother passed away when I was 13 years old. As I navigated undergraduate and graduate education, and now as I navigate my career in academia, I have always remembered the initial encouragement from my mother and how I had opportunities along the way to support and encourage other first-generation college students. As I consider my first-generation college student identity, I cannot separate it from my other social identities. I am a Black, queer, cisgender man who was raised in a Southern, low-income family. My social identities have shaped how I have had to navigate structural and internalized oppression related to racism, heterosexism, and classism and how I have benefited from privileges as a cisgender man.

Lessons Learned as a First-generation College Student

Throughout my education, I learned through subtle and overt messages that my family lacked social and cultural capital (Means et al., 2017). The subtle and overt messages led me to seek social and cultural capital outside of my family to be "successful" in education. However, as I completed my undergraduate and graduate education and began my higher education professional career, I continuously learned how these subtle and overt messages were rooted in classism and racism, specifically anti-Black racism. Reflecting now, my family and my first-generation college student identity taught me important lessons about resisting deficit perspectives and questioning dehumanizing standards that do not take into consideration one's lived experiences.

The importance of resisting deficit perspectives are ingrained in some of my earliest memories as a child becoming aware of my own social class identity. As a child, my mother received support through the Supplemental Nutrition Assistance Program (SNAP; also referred to as food stamps) after going on disability due to her Lupus diagnosis. I remember on at least one occasion being extremely embarrassed because of the glare my mother was receiving from the cashier and the people behind her for using SNAP. I remember thinking that the people at the store did not know our situation or my mother's story.

Unfortunately, I have also adopted deficit perspectives, at times, in my own work. After completing my master's program, I accepted a position at Elon University, my undergraduate alma mater. My job was to develop and implement a college access and success program for high school students with a financial need or no family history of college. When I first started working with the program, I operated from the perspective of "teaching students what they don't know." However, I quickly learned that I needed to start from the perspective of understanding what students and families in the program can teach others. I started to consider and implement approaches to work alongside students and families as they navigated pathways to postsecondary education, and students and families taught me about using agency to address social injustices and dreaming big even in the face of challenges.

My first-generation college identity taught me the importance of questioning values and standards that are not aligned with my experiences as a Black queer man who is a first-generation college student and from a low-income family. After completing my undergraduate degree, I pursued a graduate program in sociology at a large, research-intensive institution. As an undergraduate student at a small institution, I had transformational interactions with faculty members in and out of the classroom, and I wanted to replicate that as a sociology professor. However, the transition to my graduate program was a significant shock; I was told that my top priority was to focus on my research, but I was mostly drawn to teaching undergraduate students. I also wanted to conduct research in local communities to address social inequities, but I was told I should concentrate on a thesis project and should not be engaged in community-based research until later in my career. The program was not a good fit for me. I realized that as a first-generation college student I did not have good context for what it meant to choose a graduate program that reflected one's own interests and goals.

As I have navigated my career, I have frequently made decisions reflecting my values versus typically held values in academia. For example, in academia, I noticed that faculty may believe full-time doctoral students are the most interested in faculty careers compared to part-time doctoral students. I received a few offers to attend a PhD program as a full-time student, but I could not afford to live on a stipend of less than $10,000 per year, especially as someone with significant debt. I decided to work full time while pursuing my PhD. This decision was the best decision for me, even though it did not reflect the well-accepted values and standards in academia.

Being a First-generation College Student and Faculty Member

My experience as a first-generation college student, compounded by my racial and social class identities, impacts my experience as a faculty member. I have often lived by the philosophy to work twice as hard to prove an education system embedded in racism and classism wrong about my ability to become a faculty member and to earn tenure at a historically White institution. For example, I was told by senior faculty that I should aim to have two peer-reviewed publications each year to earn tenure and a promotion to associate professor. I aimed to have at least three peer-reviewed publications, leaving no doubt in anyone's mind at the institution or in the field about my ability to be successful. Although I was told that I did not need any external grants or fellowships to earn tenure and a promotion to associate professor, I submitted 15 grant proposals (11 of which were declined) in my first 5 years as a faculty member with the hopes that I could receive funding, again leaving no doubt in anyone's mind about my aptitude for success. I found myself trying to be an exceptional teacher, researcher, colleague, and community organizer to prove my place in academia (Rockquemore & Laszloffy, 2008).

This all came at the expense of sacrificing spending time with family and friends and staying focused on why I decided to become a faculty member in the first place. After earning tenure and promotion to associate professor, I noticed that I was operating again from a place of proving myself. I recently read an article by Ashley Kirkwood (2019) that argued that the idea of Black people "working twice as hard doesn't work" because of systemic barriers (para. 2). The article has inspired me to find ways to connect my research, teaching, and service back to the reasons I decided to pursue a faculty position.

I chose to become a faculty member to collaborate with youth and college students, especially racially minoritized, first-generation college, and poor and working-class youth and college students, and to address pressing local, state, and national issues through research. I have been invested in this work for over a decade. As a faculty member, I have collaborated and conducted research with high school and college students. Every summer I have worked with high school students in a college access program for students with a financial need or no family history of college in order to identify and address inequities and injustices in the United States. I find the work of reaching beyond college and university campuses to be the most profound opportunity to learn alongside youth and to collaborate with communities of young people and college students.

Given my identity as a first-generation graduate, I find it important to work on efforts to increase recruitment and retention of minoritized student populations such as racially minoritized students, first-generation college students, students from poor and working-class backgrounds, and queer and transgender students. This goal starts with being transparent and vulnerable with students about academia. For example, I share with students at the beginning of each semester how racism, classism, and other forms of oppression shape my experiences as a faculty member. I have also tried to be more explicit with students about academic jargon instead of assuming everyone has the same understanding of terms and processes related to graduate school.

Similarities and Differences Between the Authors' First-generation Faculty Paths

Although each of our stories is unique, there are common threads in the pieces of ourselves, stories/*testimonios*, and memories we shared that continue to influence how we operate in academic spaces. The value of education, for example, was instilled in all of us by family members, just in different ways. Darris' mother passed away when he was just 13 years old, but she served as the driving force behind his desire to pursue a terminal degree. Similarly, Claudia made a promise to her father when she was 5 years old, to one day live out his dream of earning a college degree. Sonja's MawMaw and PawPaw instilled in her early on that education was the best pathway to a better life. Therefore, when each of us crossed the stage after earning our PhD, we knew that we had fulfilled the dreams of our loved ones.

All three of us grew up in low-income households where we were expected to attend college. Our stories directly contradict the all-too-common stereotype that poor and working class people do not value education. In fact, this is where the nuances of our intersecting identities surface. For example, Claudia and Darris each shared a negative childhood experience that forever changed their lives. Interestingly, both experiences took place at a grocery store, where their parents were made to feel inferior. Rather than allowing these experiences to have an adverse effect on them, for both Darris and Claudia, the experiences strengthened their resolve to pursue a college degree. Sonja recognizes that, although she has White privilege, her combined marginalized identities of yielding from a working-class household and rural community, and being a first-generation college student posed significant barriers in her educational pathway.

All three of us lacked cultural capital to navigate an educational system that was not designed to help us thrive. Nevertheless, we persisted. Sometimes we felt inadequate in academic spaces because we did not fit in; other times we sought help only to feel more lost. But with each obstacle, our tenacity grew. We became better versed at navigating college even if it did not feel like it at the time. Claudia shared a common consequence first-generation college students encounter when returning home: being labeled by loved ones as "too good" or "acting White" when discussing college. Darris reflected on his journey of upholding his values above those imposed upon him by others, which has allowed him to engage in the type of work that matters to him. Sonja learned the importance of the "hustle" early on, and despite this form of capital not being recognized in academia, she constantly relies on it to navigate systemic barriers.

In writing our narratives/*testimonio*, each of us reflected on how our childhood, marginalized identities, racist/prejudice experiences, and personal values directly informed our decisions to enter the professoriate. We often reflect on the stories we shared in this chapter to remind us that education is more than a degree—it is the manifestation of our loved ones' hard work and sacrifice. Education has granted us access to spaces we had no idea existed. We are able to challenge the status quo and complicate the narrative of what it means to be a first-generation college student. We share the passion of working alongside marginalized students and the associated communities and producing the asset-based research we yearned to read as students. Nonetheless, all three of us had to work harder than continuing-generation college students and those who held more privileged social identities, feeling the pressure to prove our legitimacy within academic spaces as we constantly felt like imposters. We recognize that, as faculty members, we have the power to effect change within our departments and the courses we teach. Sonja, for example, shared that she is leading the charge in removing the GRE requirement from her program's admissions policy. She has been able to successfully articulate to colleagues and the graduate school the barriers such a requirement poses because she had to navigate similar obstacles as a student. We firmly believe that education is tied to opportunity. As faculty members we work hard to ensure not only that we create access for marginalized and minoritized students, but that, once these students arrive on campus, we advocate for them to receive an equitable education.

Finally, it is important to note that our narratives/*testimonio*, although potentially transferable to other first-generation faculty members' experiences, only represent three stories. One cannot assume the stories of other first-generation faculty mirror ours. Rather, we encourage readers to take in our stories as a starting place for awareness, understanding, and connection.

Questions for Reflection

As the authors of this chapter, we utilized a series of questions and an exercise to reflect on our personal histories as first-generation college students, our current experiences as first-generation faculty members, and our aspirations as first-generation faculty members. These questions and exercise are included here. Current faculty members and individuals who aspire to be faculty members may find these questions and the exercise helpful to engage in for individual or group reflection.

1. How do you approach/will you approach teaching, research, advising, and service to your institution and profession as a current or future faculty member?

2. If you are a first-generation college student, how does/will your first-generation identity layered with your other social identities (e.g., race, social class, gender, sexuality) shape your approach to teaching, research, advising, and service to your institution and profession as a current or future faculty member?

3. If you are a continuing generation college student, how does/will this identity layered with your other social identities (e.g., race, social class, gender, sexuality) shape your approach to teaching, research, advising, and service to your institution and profession as a current or future faculty member?

4. What messages, both positive and negative, have you learned about first-generation college students? In what ways are these messages reflected in your teaching, research,

advising, and service to your institution and profession as a current or future faculty member?

5. How, if at all, do you disrupt perpetuating deficit perspectives about first-generation college students?

As the authors of the chapter, we also used the following prompts to write our narratives or *testimonio*:

- Being a first-generation college student taught me . . .
- Given that I was a first-generation college student, as a faculty member I . . .

We found this exercise and the questions to be powerful as we considered our pathways to the professoriate as first-generation college students layered with our intersecting social identities. For current and aspiring faculty members who are first-generation college students, we offer our prompts as a strategy to reflect on your identity and how it informs your approaches to teaching, research, advising, and service to your institution and profession. We also suggest considering using your narrative as a strategy to connect with students and to invite them to share their past, current, and future experiences. We hope the questions and exercise will lead to deeper reflection about how current and future faculty members can better honor first-generation college student status as a point of pride and achievement.

References

Anzaldúa, G. (2012). *Borderlands/La frontera: The new mestiza* (4th ed.). Aunt Lute Books.

Ardoin, S. (2018). *College aspirations and access in working-class rural communities: The mixed signals, challenges, and new language first-generation students encounter.* Lexington Books.

Delgado Bernal, D. (2001). Learning and living pedagogies of the home: The mestiza consciousness of Chicana students. *International Journal of Qualitative Studies in Education, 14*(5), 623–639. https://doi.org/10.1080/09518390110059838

Delgado Bernal, D. D., Burciaga, R., & Flores Carmona, J. (2016). *Chicana/Latina testimonios as pedagogical, methodological, and activist approaches to social justice.* Routledge.

Delgado, R. (1989). Storytelling for oppositionists and others: A plea for narrative. *Michigan Law Review, 87*(8), 2411–2441. https://repository.law.umich.edu/mlr/vol87/iss8/10

García-Louis, C. (2019). Transforming the culture of academia one classroom at a time: Testimonio of a Latina junior faculty member engaging in Latina critical pedagogical activism. *Association of Mexican American Educators Journal, 13*(1), 102–123. https://doi.org/10.24974/amae.13.1.448

Gardner, S. K., & Holley, K. A. (2011). "Those invisible barriers are real": The progression of first-generation students through doctoral education. *Equity & Excellence, 44*(1), 77–92. https://doi.org/10.1080/10665684.2011.529791

Haviland, D., Ortiz, A. M., & Henriques, L. (2017). *Shaping your career: A guide for early career faculty.* Stylus.

Holley, K. A., & Gardner, S. (2012). Navigating the pipeline: How socio-cultural influences impact first-generation doctoral students. *Journal of Diversity in Higher Education, 5*(2), 112–121. https://doi.org/10.1037/a0026840

Kirkwood, A. (2019, October). Why the "working twice as hard" mentality doesn't work. *Xonecole.* https://www.xonecole.com/why-working-twice-as-hard-wont-work

Means, D. R., Beatty, C. C., Blockett, R. A., Bumbry, M., Canida, R. L., II, & Cawthon, T. W. (2017). Resilient scholars: Reflections from Black gay men on the doctoral journey. *Journal of Student Affairs Research and Practice, 54*(1), 109–120. https://doi.org/10.1080/19496591.2016.1219265

Padgett, R. D., Johnson, M. P., & Pascarella, E. T. (2012). First-generation undergraduate students and the impacts of the first year of college: Additional evidence. *Journal of College Student Development, 53*(2), 243–266. http://doi.org/10.1353/csd.2012.0032

Pérez Huber, L., & Cueva, B. M. (2016). Chicana/Latina testimonios on effects and responses to microaggressions. In D. D. Bernal, R. Burciaga, & J. Flores Carmona (Eds.), *Chicana/Latina testimonios as pedagogical, methodological, and activist approaches to social justice* (pp. 30–48). Routledge.

Rockquemore, K. A., & Laszloffy, T. (2008). *The Black academic's guide to winning tenure—Without losing your soul.* Lynne Rienner Publishers.

Shelton, L. J., & Ardoin, S. (2020). Contingent faculty/adjuncts. In M. E. David & M. J. Amey (Eds.), *The SAGE encyclopedia of higher education* (5th ed., pp. 299–301). SAGE Publications.

Soria, K. M., & Stebleton, M. J. (2012). First-generation students' academic engagement and retention. *Teaching in Higher Education, 17*(6), 673–685. https://doi.org/10.1080/1356251 7.2012.666735

Spring, J. (2016). *Deculturalization and the struggle for equality: A brief history of the education of dominated cultures in the United States (sociocultural, political, and historical studies in education)* (8th ed.). Routledge.

Toutkoushian, R. K., Stollberg, R. A., & Slaton, K. A. (2018). Talking 'bout my generation: Defining "first-generation college students" in higher education research. *Teachers College Record, 120*(4), 1–38.

Valdez, L. (1994). *Luiz Valdez early works: Actos, Bernabé and Pensameinto Serpentino.* Arte Público Press.

Vuong, M., Brown-Welty, S., & Tracz, S. (2010). The effects of self-efficacy on academic success of first-generation college sophomore students. *Journal of College Student Development, 51*(1), 50–64. https://doi.org/10.1353/csd.0.0109

10

Pathways to Senior Leadership

PATRICIA S. SMITH AND BRIAN O. HEMPHILL

In *Reframing Academic Leadership,* Bolman and Gallos (2011) stated, "Knowledge is power; and academic leaders empower themselves when they know where they are, where they want to go, and what will get them there" (p. 9). Senior leadership within the academy requires individual qualities like confidence, courage, and creativity, along with a deep understanding of the higher education landscape and its associated challenges, opportunities, politics, subtleties, and nuances. Establishing a pathway is essential for those seeking to become a senior leader, as is fully understanding that "every institution of higher education is unique, but all have much in common" (Bolman & Gallos, 2011, p. 4).

The commonalities of Western higher education help establish the basic steps toward senior leadership. However, the uniqueness of each institution belies the culture and traditions at play, which senior leaders must understand and acknowledge to truly become successful—including finding the best institutional fit in which to serve. Fit may seem elusive to first-generation aspiring senior leaders. Yet, gaining insight into aligning one's skill set with institutional distinctions such as public or private, 4-year or 2-year, minority serving, gender specific, faith based, and so on, is essential to successfully setting a path to senior leadership. Identifying the desire to become a senior leader is the "where you want to go" Bolman and Gallos referred to. Developing a pathway is the "how you will get there." The "where you are" component reflects the life varying journeys leading to the point of aspiring to become a senior leader.

Mid-Level Career Goals Accomplished: Now What?

Reaching mid-level career goals takes persistence and resilience—hallmarks of successful first-generation professionals. Once mid-level goals are accomplished, one might question, "Now what?" For some, the next step is pursuing senior leadership. This, too, takes persistence and resilience. Preparing to seek a senior leadership position also requires multiple other components, such as self-reflection, planning, and adaptability.

Self-Reflection

Self-reflection in the context of developing a pathway to senior leadership allows one to identify strengths and assets while also identifying growth opportunities. For aspiring first-generation senior leaders, self-reflection has likely already included evaluating the influence of such constructs as imposter syndrome (as referenced in Chapter 2 of this book) and familial expectations (as referenced by several authors in this book). Joshi and Mangette (2018) discussed the interconnectedness of imposter syndrome with mental health components, such as anxiety and depression, and stated the "imposter exhibits workaholic behaviors that lead to exhaustion and increase the risk of burnout [and] the rewards and recognition from their work is then associated with anxiety, stress, and work-life balance issues" (p. 5). As one aspires to become a senior leader, self-reflection should certainly include how work and life are integrated, how to manage stress and anxiety, and how to keep a healthy balance of juggling multiple and competing priorities.

Parkman (2016) stated, "In the mind of the imposter, a very positive but very false impression of ability has been created. . . . Imposterism, at its root, is about an inability to accurately self-assess" (p. 52). To progress into senior leadership, a true, deep understanding of ability and capacity must be individually solidified, along with a strong sense of self. This does not mean one may no longer feel like an imposter. Rather, through mentors, coaches, and trusted colleagues, strengths and assets are affirmed (and reaffirmed), and growth opportunities are quantified to inform competency development and skill building.

Self-reflection is not a one-and-done process. Rather, self-assessment is an ongoing process. Components of self-reflection may remain consistent, but realizations and outcomes may change over time. Professional growth certainly plays a part in why insights and results may change over the course of one's career. Professional self-reflection may be influenced by work experiences, supervisors and colleagues, challenges and successes, and spontaneous "aha" moments. However, do not overlook how personal experiences may also influence professional self-reflection and growth. Becoming a parent, a partner, facing illness, and taking care of an elderly parent or family member are all examples of life experiences that may also shape growth toward senior leadership positions.

First-generation aspiring leaders may not see around them blended or balanced examples of work–life integration. This issue is well documented within academia. For example, for female faculty, parenting or caregiving can take time away from pursuing tenure. Others may forgo wellness goals to accept additional projects and opportunities in the workplace. The challenge of balance is one of many reasons why a solid support system of mentors and trusted colleagues is helpful in establishing a pathway to senior leadership. If work–life integration is not a strength within a mentor's own experience, the mentor can likely help aspiring leaders find others with that skill to help model integrated, successful leadership navigation.

An example of successful work–life integration is bringing one's partner to campus events. Another example is including one's children in age- and content-appropriate campus activities, such as family weekend, homecoming, and commencement. Sharing the public aspects of the administrative experience may help address time spent away from families while also exemplifying for junior staff an appropriate example of blending life and work. In contemporary times, with the growing push for authentic leadership requiring deep self-relfection, finding a genuine work–life balance allows aspiring leaders to develop both in and out of the office.

Another component of self-reflection is assessing one's leadership abilities. These assessments not only provide a sense of one's leadership capacity and preferred styles but also help guide career goals and provide a shared language to deepen relationship building within and across teams. Several leadership assessment tools are available, some free and some not. Each tool has strengths and drawbacks. Using multiple tools, however, can give a fuller picture of one's leadership abilities. This may be particularly helpful to those experiencing self-doubt or imposter syndrome. Completing tools at different points in one's career may also illuminate growth and shifts in capacity as new, more challenging opportunities arise and are successfully navigated, and as one's professional sense of self solidifies.

Whether seeking feedback about unconscious or implicit bias, personality, individual strengths, or leadership style, there is an assessment tool for it. Often, feedback mechanisms within leadership assessments provide a summary of strengths and weaknesses. Such feedback helps shape leadership development plans. It is often easier, and more comfortable, to rely on and enhance the strengths within one's skill set. However, an essential component of creating a pathway to senior leadership through self-reflection and assessment is to also identify areas of weakness and determine ways to strengthen those capacities.

Leadership assessment and self-reflection is broader than completing online tools. Bolman and Gallos (2011) described four habits for leadership effectiveness, which are salient within leadership assessment: consistently seeking feedback from others, reliably testing assumptions, seeking balance between advocacy and inquiry, and understanding the theories and frameworks used to inform daily work.

Bolman and Gallos (2011) stated, "Leadership lies in the eyes of the beholder—and if academic leadership don't know how their constituents see them, they're in trouble" (p. 41). As such, when seeking feedback, aspiring senior leaders should be proactive, persistent, appreciative, and open to critical comments. A risk in seeking honest feedback is feeling hurt or discouraged by what others have to say. However, in using clear and consistent messaging, along with remaining calm, nondefensive, and gracious, those aspiring to senior leadership positions help model and exemplify to individuals providing feedback that honesty truly is desired and valued—as does taking action to address, fix, and strengthen areas for which constructive criticism has been provided.

Remaining gracious also accompanies testing one's assumptions. It is easy to make assumptions about why individuals say or do things that do not align with one's own beliefs and perceptions. Everyone has biases that frame how they view experiences and circumstances. Rather than assuming, it helps to ask others what they meant by a particular comment, how they are experiencing or perceiving a situation, or what they intended with a specific behavior or action. This is certainly easier said than done. Testing assumptions does not just help the aspiring senior leader grow, however. Exemplifying testing assumptions helps those they are working with learn and grow as well.

Through self-assessment, aspiring senior leaders may determine if they maintain a balance between *inquiry*—seeking to learn and better understand, to strengthen leadership ability over time—and *advocacy*—speaking up to make a change or dynamic shift immediately or as swiftly as possible. For some, this balance is a challenge. Successful inquiry takes strength in listening, building trust, and developing rapport. The act of inquiry, for some, feels like a low-risk activity, using skills one is already comfortable with, along with the potential for low to high reward. Successful advocacy takes confidence, data, and opportunity. Advocating, for some, feels like a high-risk activity, as it involves inviting judgement and scrutiny, with the potential for a high reward or a low reward. Put another way, advocating may make for quick wins and inquiry may make for longer-term wins. Aspiring senior leaders must be capable in both regards.

On the path to academic senior leadership, it is common to field questions about what theories or framework one uses to inform their understanding of student development and student success. Such questions provide the opportunity to address how one's daily work is informed by theoretical constructs, as well as to express how one's leadership reflects such constructs. Those aspiring to senior leadership should be well versed in applying theories to the various components within higher education leadership, and readily able to articulate and demonstrate how a particular theory informs one's work. Put another way, although leadership to some extent revolves around trusting one's gut or instincts, leadership efforts should also be grounded in and informed by theory, data, assessment, and outcomes.

Planning

After thoughtful self-reflection, one can begin to identify and plan their individualized path to senior leadership. Aspiring senior leaders need to ask themselves whether they can gain the requisite experiences they desire or need at their current institution and in their current position. If not, they must determine if they need to relocate—through a lateral move or promotion, or through pursuing an advanced degree.

Those who are able to relocate might gain broader experiences, more quickly. However, doing so may also raise questions about one's long-term commitment when seeking another position, if one's résumé or curriculum vita reflects multiple moves over short periods of time. What is construed as "short periods of time" may shift over one's career. For example, residence life professionals often work 2 to 3 years in a position before moving into a mid-level role. This is not considered a brief period of time for residential staff. Alternately, serving as a director for 2 years at one institution and then moving on to a different institution could very well be considered as moving on too quickly. Those who move up the ladder within an existing institution might seemingly reflect commitment more strongly, yet may take longer to gain depth and breadth of experiences. For example, one who has served as an assistant director, director, and assistant vice president at a single institution will likely be viewed as committed. However, when competing against applicants for a vice presidency at another institution, some may argue the candidate's experience is limited, and it is important to note that successful senior leaders have already traveled both paths.

Relocating to a new institution requires a game plan for personal and professional integration. Professionally, it is important to establish an understanding of the culture, norms, and expectations of a new campus community. A common mistake for new leaders is trying to make their mark too quickly, before they understand what is considered sacred and untouchable at their new institution. One way to gain a depth and breadth of knowledge about a new campus community is to schedule time to meet with colleagues. During these meetings, the new senior leader should ask questions to learn about what the institution does exceptionally well, what is unique and revered for the campus, and what change is needed to help the institution thrive.

Additional due diligence is essential if relocating means moving to a new community. Search online, if unable to visit much before moving, to identify the resources, businesses, and services essential to a successful move. These may include identifying a place of worship, medical care, pet care, dry cleaning, a hair stylist, and so on. Whether big or small, whatever day-to-day needs can be addressed before moving will remove some of the stress and anxiety of starting somewhere new. Whenever possible, try to build in a few weeks between positions, particularly when moving, to allow time to establish the day-to-day routines necessary to have a smooth transition. When considering a move, one may also need to think about the impact of relocating on those around them, such as partners, children, and extended families. What will one's partner do in a new community? Will one's children have readily available afterschool programs and care providers? What commitments and obligations to extended family does one have?

In addition to gaining professional experiences to support navigating a path to senior leadership, educational experiences are essential as well. According to the American Council on Education, in 2017, 77% of male and 86% of female postsecondary presidents held a doctorate degree. As stated by Eddy and Garza Mitchell (2017), an advanced degree is the "currency" needed for senior leaders. For nonfaculty senior leaders, academic partners will see those with a terminal degree as a qualified peer more frequently than those without a terminal degree.

The process of earning a doctoral degree facilitates the development of scholars and practitioners who can discover, utilize, and disseminate knowledge. Obtaining an advanced degree also facilitates the development of numerous transferable, administrative skills, such as disciplinary knowledge, teaching experience, and intersecting expertise with societal need, to name just a few. However, barriers remain for first-generation individuals seeking an advanced degree. Hostile campus climates, entrenched curricula and pedagogy fostering unintentional negative learning through reinforcing the status quo and majority viewpoint, and exclusionary practices contribute to underrepresented individuals not pursuing or stepping out of the pursuit of an advanced degree (Gasman et al., 2015). Having a strong and solid network of mentors, coaches, and trusted allies can assist first-generation aspiring senior leaders in sticking to their professional (and academic) goals.

Although there is a traditional preference in academia for earning degrees back to back, going straight from undergraduate to graduate to doctoral work without a break is not the only path. For first-generation leaders, back-to-back pursuit of degrees may not be feasible for myriad reasons, be they familial, financial, or personal wellness. As such, a critical next step for aspiring senior leaders who have successfully met mid-level goals without an advanced degree is determining how to best pursue one.

Aspiring senior leaders should determine if earning an advanced degree at one's current institution is an option. Is there supervisory support in doing so? If there is support but no viable program option, are there collaborative programs within the region? What about summer-based, time-limited cohort programs? Does the current employing institution offer tuition discounts or leave hours to pursue educational goals?

If one's employing institution or regional institutions do not provide an advanced degree option, online education is another possibility. Online advanced educational programs have grown in recent years, gaining attention for national rankings, affordability, and accessibility. Although in-person doctoral programs have historically garnered more favor within higher education, there are online, accredited programs from well-established, well-regarded institutions and these programs have destigmatized the pursuit of online education. Due diligence is required for researching online programs. As with in-person programs, online programs have myriad components to consider, such as in-state/out-of-state cost, cohort experiences, the ability to complete the program solely online, program length, previous degree requirements, and part-time versus full-time requirements.

Aspiring senior leaders must also determine whether working while earning a degree is a necessity. If briefly stepping away from full-time work is an option, working part time while completing full-time coursework may be possible. An assistantship during program completion might be another option. There is no one right way to earn an advanced degree—only what is right for the person striving to do so.

When committing to an advanced degree, aspiring senior leaders must also determine what degree to seek. Historically, the Doctor of Philosophy has been the pinnacle of doctoral degrees for senior leaders. However, a rising number of senior leaders hold a Doctor of Education (Johnson, 2017). As stated by Freeman and Kochan (2012), senior leaders "come from a variety of academic backgrounds. It is important to note that there is no degree that places a person on a linear track to [senior leadership]. What is generally recognized is that graduate education plays a vital role in developing academic leaders" (p. 94).

Adaptability

The ability to adapt is key for all senior leaders. Senior leaders face two competing demands: executing to meet today's challenges while adapting to meet the challenges of tomorrow. Eddy and Garza Mitchell (2017) defined *adaptability* for aspiring senior leaders as the ability to "transform their own notions of leading before being able to lead transformational change" (p. 130).

An increased capacity to adapt comes from actively exploring and experimenting with new ideas and different ways to reach objectives (Zaccaro & Banks, 2004). One way to gain adaptability is to employ contingency thinking. Based on the construct that there is no best way to manage a situation, contingency thinking allows decision makers to acknowledge that all situations are different and fluid, and that the tasks at hand may influence decisions at different points in time. Contingency thinking provides the structure to pivot when necessary, and reflects being solution focused. One path toward strengthening contingency thinking capacity is to quantify at least two solutions for every one problem identified.

Another way to frame adaptability through contingency thinking is to think of creating or identifying preparedness plans. Preparedness plans exist for crisis management, facilities, and technology. Although such plans take proactive measures, they are most often used in reactive ways. Adaptability and contingency thinking utilize proactive measures to contemplate alternatives and possibilities. Contingency thinking fosters a forward-thinking, solution-focused mindset while also demonstrating resilience, persistence, and reliability.

Mentors can support aspiring leaders in expanding their adaptability capacity. Mentors also support those aspiring to senior leadership through helping them see beyond what is right in front of them—to imagine more than what seems feasible in the present moment. In addition to providing professional and personal support, mentors can offer guidance, sponsor additional opportunities, and increase one's visibility within the industry (Hill & Wheat, 2017). The capacity to employ adaptability is useful as a tool for navigating bureaucracy and politics. Mentors can also buffer mentees from "overt and covert forms of discrimination, lend legitimacy to a person of position, [and] provide guidance and training in the political operation of the organization" (Schipani et al., 2009, p. 100).

The politics of leadership in higher education are ever-present. One of the keys to navigating politics is listening. Through listening, aspiring senior leaders can identify alliances and relationships, gain understanding of organizational structures and pitfalls, and quantify potential next steps—all without getting entrenched in the bureaucracy that exists in all institutions of higher education. Mentors, then, can help provide a safe space to process what one learns, and to float ideas in a low-risk environment. In successfully reaching mid-level goals, aspiring leaders have already demonstrated at least some ability to navigate politics and bureaucracy.

Be the Leader You Want to Be

Through the course of one's career, leadership lessons arise in myriad ways. Mentors may deliver overt messages such as staying true to one's core values, leading with compassion and care, and embracing adaptability. Other lessons will arise through day-to-day practices. For example, simply listening to and observing how others lead will reveal traits to emulate and model, such as reflecting respect and fairness, embracing a team approach, and constantly seeking to learn and grow.

Leadership lessons also become evident when leadership styles do not align. Interacting across those differences and modeling authentic leadership opens the door for aspiring senior leaders to progress in their careers. When leadership styles do not align, it can become tempting to pull back or disengage. Instead, lean into the difference and commit to a shift in mindset. Embrace the ethos of never being outworked. Such a perspective helps prepare aspiring senior leaders to take the next step when the opportunity arises.

Being the leader one aspires to be takes confidence. Everyone makes mistakes and stumbles. Being a senior leader requires making difficult decisions, and some difficult decisions may result in disappointing outcomes. Acknowledging this disappointment without taking it personally is key for successful senior leaders. Successful senior leaders must know where they are and who they are, where they want to go and why, and what will get them there.

Learning Beyond the Classroom: The Role of Lifelong Learning

Higher education is a learning enterprise. Along with understanding the mission of higher education as centered on teaching and learning, higher education professionals should also embrace the frame of a learning organization as referenced by Senge (1990). Senge described a learning organization as one with continuous efforts to expand capacity, nurture creativity, and commit to intellectual curiosity, all in the pursuit of a collective aspiration. Senior leaders must thus personally pledge to and strategically drive the pursuit of lifelong learning. First-generation aspiring senior leaders who commit to this learning framework will be poised to embrace myriad, diverse professional opportunities as they emerge.

Embracing Opportunities: Depth and Breadth of Experiences

According to a 2016 National Association of Colleges and Employers survey, first-generation college graduates apply for and accept fewer jobs than do non-first-generation graduates (Eismann, 2016). This is, in part, due to first-generation graduates feeling unqualified, even though they have very similar qualifications to their non-first-generation peers. First-generation higher education leaders must push past this perspective to gain the experiences necessary for senior leadership.

Each position that one holds will present new challenges; deepen specific competencies; and offer different perspectives on innovation, change, student learning, and organizational behavior. Lateral moves, in addition to short-term or interim positions, should be explored as an opportunity to stretch and deepen skill sets as well as to understand issues from the perspective of a new seat.

Moving through mid-level management toward senior positions will require one to supervise and make decisions for departments and areas for which they have not had direct experience. In order to be prepared for those opportunities, it is important to reflect on transferrable skills such as budgeting, supervision, time management, delegation, program management, and assessment; participate in collaborative endeavors that expand exposure to other areas; build relationships across the field; and stay abreast of issues that deeply impact other functional units, such as the impact of mental illness, food insecurity, and shifting student demographics on college student success.

Types of institutions: An opportunity to develop breadth. Every institution type can provide a new lens through which to view similar issues. For example, funding models may vary. The source of revenue for the institution will impact how a senior leader makes decisions and spends time. Human resource functions vary by state, and often within a state. Serving a large, public, land-grant institution illuminates different ways of thinking about the student experience versus serving a midsize, private institution. The approach will vary based on student demographics, resources, and mission. Regardless of the type of institution one ultimately wishes to serve, individual leadership capacity is tremendously enhanced by working at a variety of institution types.

Committee work: Increasing understanding across the institution. Committee work is a great way to garner deeper understanding of complex issues, stakeholders, and university processes. Default to saying "yes" when offered to serve on committees. When not directly asked, when a faculty member, colleague, or constituent is working on a task force that seems interesting, seek to become involved. After serving on search committees, seek to chair one search committee to increase the understanding of human resource procedures beyond the candidate screening process. Each of these short-term experiences expands one's network and allows a glimpse into another facet of an institution. After reaching personal learning capacity on a particular committee, step away and suggest that a junior colleague be nominated so that they may in turn develop those skills.

Community engagement: Exploring partnership and shared commitments. Community engagement and external partnerships are critical to success for senior leaders in higher education. As written by Hamrick et al. (2002), "Colleges were founded to offer an educational experience for young men preparing to become leaders in their community" (p. 4). Although participants engaging with higher education have expanded beyond the singular demographic and community is now considered in the global context, the mission for preparing leaders still exists. Therefore, it is important for senior leaders to serve on town-gown boards and engage with town councils, local schools, nonprofits, area employers, and landlords, for example. These relationships will help to develop relevant fiscal, environmental, and development strategies within the academy to meet shared aspirations of both the institution and the surrounding community.

Short- and long-term tactics: Thinking "now" and "later." Crimmin and Dobrowski (2016) wrote, "Institutional leaders must be visionary in their approach and strategic in their thinking" (p. 63). The capacity to align short-term tactics and long-term strategic planning is integral to the success of senior leaders. Developing the skill to connect tactics and strategies should be an explicit goal for all first-generation leaders as they develop a pathway to senior leadership. One might begin by examining current individual work and connecting every program and outcome to the institutional strategic plan. Examine the plan for gaps, then design, propose, and deliver tactics that fill each gap. Listening, collaboration, innovation, and a strong process will contribute to achieving the targeted goal of affiliating short-term methods with long-term strategic achievements.

Ongoing Competency Development and Skill Building

Higher education is not stagnant, and thus, neither are successful senior leaders. Kezar and Holcombe (2017) stated, in the "current era of significant change in higher education, there is growing attention to the importance of understanding the leadership required to guide campuses successfully" (p. 1), as well as how those requirements are influenced by the various constituencies senior leaders serve. As such, a planned pathway to senior leadership must include mechanisms to enhance requisite competencies and strengthen leadership skills. Broadly speaking, in addition to an evidenced commitment to student success and demonstrated leadership capacity, senior leaders consistently need strong communication skills, the ability to build relationships both on and off campus, strategic planning and assessment savvy, capacity for conflict and crisis management, and legislative insight.

Communication skills. Ruben et al. (2017) aptly stated, "Every communication encounter has the potential to convey information and to shape the kind of relationships that develop" (p. 205). Miscommunication may lead to confusion, defensiveness, low morale, loss of confidence, and disengagement from team members and constituents; effective communication may elicit buy-in and support from skeptical employees, sway adversaries to allies, and move the needle on student success. Senior leaders are required to communicate formally and informally, verbally and in writing, through various online platforms, publicly and privately, and in sharing successes and failures. Thus, the value and importance of strong and strategic communication capacity cannot be overstated.

Strategic communication includes being clear about the goals of communication, the intended audience, and the desired message. A solid foundation of trust and understanding within intended audiences further strengthens communication, and yet effective strategic messages typically need to be shared and received multiple times to truly be heard. Communication that is memorable and sharable is often the most impactful. Although there is certainly value added through dynamic and engaging communicators, there is also strength through communicators that offer quiet consistency; rapport building; and an evidenced ability to listen just as much, if not more so, than speaking.

Relationship building. Just as strong, intentional, and strategic communication skills are essential to becoming a successful senior leader, so is the ability to develop relationships both on and off campus. Dungy and Ellis (2011) asserted that senior leaders must have interpersonal skills that facilitate interaction with a wide array of constituents, as well as the capacity to express a narrative that speaks to all of those constituents. Put another way, in a day's work, senior leaders interact with students, faculty, and staff, as well as board members, alumni, business leaders, community leaders, and politicians. Senior leaders must find ways to collaborate and develop partnerships that are intentionally developed, purposeful to the work of the institution, and beneficial to each of the parties involved.

A capacity for relationship building comes about in multiple ways. Ruben et al. (2017) expressed relationship building as gaining respect and influence through such actions as developing a reputation for integrity, discretion, reliability, and helpfulness; keeping one's word; committing to the common good; being genuine and authentic; always being prepared; welcoming multiple perspectives; evidencing humility; and mentoring as well as being mentored. First-generation aspiring senior leaders have likely already developed these traits in reaching their mid-level goals.

Assessment and strategic planning. An evidenced ability to build relationships helps lend confidence in the ever-increasing scrutiny of accountability within Western higher education. Another trait successful senior leaders possess, particularly related to accountability, is a strong capacity for assessment and strategic planning. Assessment and data analysis provide practical benefits for driving student success, such as through program development, prioritization efforts, and allocation of fiscal resources. Strategic planning does the same. Kimbrough (2011) described how senior leaders must be engaged with assessment, strategic planning, and national studies, not only as a component of accountability, but also as an essential component of data-driven and data-informed decision making.

Strategic planning in higher education has gained attention for serving as a leadership tool, designed to set "future organizational direction in a dynamic environment through a process that takes account of—and ideally engages—key stakeholders" (Ruben et al., 2017, p. 225). Senior leaders are most successful in their strategic planning when such planning is considered within a regional and global context; informed by ambitious yet achievable and clearly narrated goals; and informed by a foundation and framework for decision making, program planning and prioritization, and fiscal allocations. Aspiring senior leaders may already have the opportunity to engage in strategic planning as a component of their current position. If not, they might gain experience through involvement with professional organizations or working with local/community agencies. However they gain the experience, aspiring senior leaders must be able to demonstrate capacity with and deep understanding of successful strategic planning and the myriad roles of assessment within higher education, such as accreditation, accountability, and program prioritization.

Conflict management. Aspiring senior leaders must be able to successfully manage conflict. Bolman and Gallos (2011) stated the goal of conflict management "is not to eliminate conflict [as] not all disagreements can be fully resolved" (p. 130). Rather, the goal is to establish processes for individuals to safely learn and grow through differences. Bolman and Gallos (2011) went on to describe how senior leaders can best manage conflict through focusing on changing their own actions, looking to learn rather than avoid or fix, and seeking to see the big picture.

Heifetz and Linsky (2002) described how senior leaders put themselves on the line when they "tell people what they need to hear rather than what they want to hear. Although [senior leaders] may see with clarity and passion a promising future of progress and gain, people will see with equal passion the losses" (p. 12) such leaders are asking them to sustain. Sometimes, leaders invite conflict by making difficult and challenging decisions, which includes risk taking. According to Dukes (2011), "It is always easier to defend controversial decisions if they have been made on the basis of sound research, with fairness, and in a collaborative manner" (p. 213). Managing conflict, as with risk taking, requires the ability to listen, a willingness to consider multiple perspectives, and a focus on the greater good. Both managing conflict and risk taking are necessary components of serving as a successful senior leader.

Crisis management. In the wake of increasing campus violence, racially charged incidences, free speech protests, and political confrontations, senior leaders must be proactively prepared to manage crises. It is no longer a matter of if a crisis will occur; rather, it is a matter of when a crisis will occur and how prepared senior leaders are to manage during the maelstrom and afterward. As such, aspiring senior leaders must have capacity and confidence with crisis management.

The speed in which critical information is disseminated to various constituencies is a significant factor in assessing the success of crisis communication (Lawson, 2007) and, ultimately, gauging the success of crisis management. Olsen (2017) stated, "Public perception has become reality—reputations are made and destroyed overnight thanks to the power of social and online media and an emboldened public" (para. 1). Not only must aspiring senior leaders have crisis management experience, they must also have the capacity to offer clarity, calm, and community care to various constituencies during and after a crisis.

For those without crisis management in their portfolio, myriad opportunities abound to gain experience. Seek to engage with the institutional crisis management team. Assist with case management at both an individual and event level and at-risk outreach. Participate in behavioral intervention teams. Volunteer for tabletop exercises. Seek training opportunities. Keep in mind, crisis management capacity comes with proactive planning and practice.

Legislative insight. Public higher education in the United States is primarily funded through a combination of student tuition and state legislative appropriations (Deming & Figlio, 2016). As such, it is essential for aspiring senior leaders to gain legislative experience. Such experience increases one's capacity to appropriately engage and advocate as a senior leader. Legislative experience, however, must go beyond the fiscal aspects. Higher education, both public and private, is also informed and shaped by state policy and legislation.

During the 2019 state legislative sessions, 502 bills were enacted across the country addressing postsecondary education matters. Nearly 50% of the 502 bills focused on fiscal and affordability issues (National Conference of State Legislatures, 2019). Examples of topics reflected in the 2019 legislation include the use of targeted tax credits within specific higher education institutions, community college districting, degree completion rates, scholarships and loans, university governance, campus safety, student mental health, and tuition and fee structures. These examples demonstrate the need for aspiring senior leaders to have broad legislative experience. For those whose portfolio does not include legislative responsibilities or components, experience may be sought through such actions as shadowing an institutional point person for legislative matters, traveling to general sessions to observe the governance process, and participating with advocacy days. Experience may also be gained through engaging with professional organizations that support national advocacy days, as well as organizations that advocate on behalf of institutions.

Developing Financial Acumen

After the housing crisis of 2008, the "financial underpinnings that supported higher education for generations weakened considerably" (Selingo, 2015, p. 6). Many of the components of successfully serving as a senior leader in higher education have thus become even more challenging. Challenges include fundraising in a growingly competitive market and creating or identifying new financial revenue streams. Financial models for higher education have shifted. From navigating decreased state funding to managing increased expectations for return on investment, financial acumen is a necessity for aspiring senior leaders. Stewardship of public funds, managing complex budgets, and fundraising are necessary skills for leaders to develop.

Complex budget management. The viability of any institution of higher education begins with sound budget management. Those aspiring to senior leadership, thus, must have the requisite skills to navigate intricate, multifaceted budgets. Experience with budgets most commonly is gained from work experience, but experience may also be gained through working with community agencies, serving professional organizations, via coursework, or through volunteering in foundations or on boards.

Aspiring senior leaders must be able to demonstrate that they are responsible stewards of fiscal resources. They must be able to quantify sound decision making while identifying efficiencies and growing revenue. Grant writing, creating campus partnerships, and streamlining costs are all feasible opportunities to gain experience with budgets within mid-level administration. As job responsibilities grow, budgets often grow with them. Establishing strong and consistent budget practices with smaller budgets sets a solid foundation for stepping into bigger and more complex budgets.

Fundraising. Fundraising is considered an essential element for presidents in particular, and increasingly for other senior leaders in higher education. According to the Deloitte Center for Higher

Education Excellence (2017), surveyed presidents of postsecondary institutions identified fundraising skill development as the number one professional training opportunity they needed. In addition to overall fundraising capacity, senior leaders need to embrace multiple mechanisms for fundraising. For example, although telephone campaigns once drove fundraising efforts, today, a multifaceted and integrated approach is needed.

Donors are waiting longer periods of time post-graduation before they consistently give, and fewer are donating at all. Online platforms have grown, making crowd-funding and social campaigns increasingly viable. However, donors ultimately give to people, not platforms, thus the rise in terms such as friend-raising in place of fundraising, to underscore the need of connecting individual donor passions and interests with institutional needs and program specific campaigns. Aspiring senior leaders need to find ways to engage with fundraising efforts, such as volunteering with an existing campaign or aligning with campus partners. Fundraisers must be "highly skilled at matching donor interests to institutional needs" (Bowman, 2010, p. 23).

Professional Engagement and Academic Contributions

Building a path to senior leadership does not end with building competency and skill. Aspiring senior leaders must professionally engage beyond campus and contribute academically through teaching, research, and scholarship. This is because academic leaders have a responsibility and duty to give back to the profession. Contributing professionally and academically are ways in which to serve and share talents based on professional and personal experiences, and lay the foundation for other first-generation leaders to find their way.

Professional engagement and academic contributions take on many forms, such as leadership development, and research and publishing. Active membership within professional organizations, for example, helps aspiring leaders develop their professional identity, provides opportunities to engage with leadership off campus, advances one's understanding of various components within higher education, informs standards and best practices, strengthens networks, and enhances skill building. Contributing to the scholarship of learning, student development, or an individual area of study may come in the form of publishing, teaching, or conference presentations.

Leadership development. In 2017, higher education presidents indicated that leadership development was the second most pressing training needed to be a successful senior leader, trailing only fundraising (Deloitte Center for Higher Education Excellence, 2017). However, these presidents also indicated little opportunity for or engagement in such training. Historically, academic leadership (and the pursuit of such) has been viewed as taking away from the purpose of higher education: teaching, learning, and research.

Ruben et al. (2017) stated, "Many of the principles of effective leadership proven to be of value in other sectors receive little emphasis in higher education" (p. 3). They went on to assert that applying such principles is critical for advancing institutions of higher education. As such, aspiring senior leaders should find ways to engage in personal and professional leadership development, whether formal or informal.

Research and publishing. Aspiring senior leaders whose leadership paths have not been through perceived traditional routes, such as within academic affairs, should also find ways to contribute academically. Research, writing, and publishing are all examples of ways in which to do so. For senior leaders, research can "illuminate areas that need improvement and serve as catalysts for new programs" (Dukes, 2011, p. 213), as well as help translate work from one area of campus to another and give back to the field and the profession.

Translating research into publications disseminates insight and lessons learned beyond the campus community, as well as brings attention to the institution. Publishing helps aspiring senior leaders further develop communication skills, contribute professionally, and even build relationships with readers and aspiring leaders. Those seeking to grow in the realm of academic contributions can start with such actions as completing book reviews, blogging, and contributing to professional organization newsletters. Coauthoring is another opportunity. This is a way in which mentors and mentees can work together to strengthen one another's work.

Lift as you climb. Aspiring senior leaders should not forget where they came from. One way to do so is to lift others up while climbing toward individual goals. This concept can also be framed as managing as well as leading. Just as aspiring senior leaders rely on trusted mentors and networks to help guide their ascent to senior leadership, they should foster similar guidance and support for those they are currently leading.

The new professionals of today are tomorrow's senior leaders. Build staff by helping them acquire the skills they are missing. Involve up-and-coming staff with proactive learning opportunities, such as coauthoring a chapter, as well as difficult decision making, such as listening in on a phone call during which challenging news will be delivered. Such opportunities demonstrate to new staff that they, too, may aspire to senior leadership some day.

More Than the First-generation Identity: Incorporating Intersectionality

In 1989, Kimberlé Crenshaw, a law professor at the University of California, Los Angeles, introduced the term *intersectionality* to highlight the marginalization of Black women in law, politics, and theory (Carbado et al., 2013). Many have come to understand the concept of how oppression is connected across identities. This concept, originally calling attention to race and gender, has expanded to include sexual orientation, gender identity, gender expression, age, class, nationality, veteran status, disability, religion, size, and a continuing evolution of other identity markers. Although first-generation status is relatively new to the conversation around marginalization, it is important to consider how this identity intertwines with other identities to potentially impact individuals in similar and distinct ways.

Gender. The term *glass ceiling* describes the plateau often faced by women who aspire to become senior leaders (Johnson, 2017). This concept enhances understanding of the "intangible systemic barriers" that inhibit women from reaching the highest levels of leadership (Johnson, 2017, p. 6). Consider the informal networking that is important to advancement. Although expectations are rarely explicit, the activities—like golf outings or other sporting events—may be culturally quite masculine. The event itself is rarely the issue, however. Rather, women who choose to not participate in these activities miss out on relationship building, insights, and cues about future decisions in the organization. Of course, this is also true for any individual who simply has different interests or obligations.

Johnson (2017) further stated that among the faculty ranks in higher education, there also exists a "pipeline myth" (p. 4), which is the fallacy of too few qualified women as an explanation for the lack of women in leadership positions. In truth, the pipeline has done a tremendous job of training more than enough women for leadership in higher education. "For example, female students have earned half or more of all baccalaureate degrees for the past three decades and of all doctoral degrees for almost a decade" (Johnson, 2017, p. 4). These data call higher education professionals to consider their own advocacy for the success of women and should encourage further critique and improvements to the structures to support equity within administrative organizations in higher education.

Sexual orientation, gender identity, and gender expression. Charles R. Middleton (2016), who launched the organization

LGBTQ Presidents in Higher Education, shared, "At the dawn of the new millennium, to the best of our knowledge, there were only two openly LGBTQ presidents. Today, there are over 70—hardly a monumental shift but progress nonetheless" (para. 3). In 2014, the Association of Governing Boards of Universities and Colleges released five recommendations for change in higher education to help protect LGBTQIA+ students, faculty, and staff (Trammell, 2014).

Certainly, organizations and recommendations are important for the success of LGBTQIA+ individuals seeking senior leadership positions in higher education. However, it is equally imperative that professionals who do not identify as LGBTQIA+ take note of the challenges within their organizations and do their part to sustain meaningful change. A shift toward greater expectations of inclusion has assisted in increased visibility of LGBTQIA+ individuals. Policies related to pronoun use, preferred names, family and partner benefits, health care, and more should accompany strident efforts of LGBTQIA+ affirming campus cultures and climates.

Race. According to a 2017 study by the American Council on Education, only 17% of college presidents were racial minorities. Today, people of color make up 45% of the undergraduate student body across all U.S. institutions (Brown, 2019). However, only one fifth of college faculty and staff are people of color. The College and University Professional Association for Human Resources shares ample data regarding both representation and salary equity concerns for people of color in the academy (McChesney, 2018).

Faculty and staff of color and indigenous faculty and staff also carry the burden of uncompensated and invisible labor related to their identities (Matthew, 2016). This labor may come in the form of advising multicultural student organizations; serving on search committees that seek a "diverse" voice; sitting on panels to educate their peers; and networking with diverse alumni, board members, and prospective students. These are essential functions within the academy, and higher education institutions benefit from having diverse representation in these (and all) spaces. Smaller representation of diverse individuals means that the load of this work is distributed among a smaller group and the negative impact is greater.

Family status and role. Higher education professionals may also face unique circumstances that present barriers to their advancement based on family responsibilities. For example, caring for an aging parent may require being out of the office during the workday. Raising children may limit the number of evenings available to attend campus events. Providing a single income for a family may limit the number of pro bono opportunities in which one can engage.

Although this list of identities is certainly not exhaustive, deeper examination helps generate questions of the importance of community for people with diverse backgrounds. Additionally, senior leaders should consider the benefits of mentorship across and among identities. Higher education systems should nurture success for all people, including those with experiences related to invisible identities. Considering experiences at the intersections of identities offers a more nuanced understanding of the lived experiences of diverse leaders, as evidenced in *The Table: Stories From Black Women in Student Affairs* (Abdulahad et al., 2018). This text offers stories of the trials faced by women of color in the academy. Self-reflection around personal identities will both nurture authentic leadership and create inclusive, successful senior leaders in higher education.

Self-Understanding: Authentically Aligned Leadership

Intentional, effective leadership will be achieved only through authentic alignment of talents, purpose, experience, style, and vision. A strong understanding of one's own strengths, leadership style, and goals is only a portion of the equation for successful senior leaders.

Although leaders can do well without alignment, excellence will be within reach if one's strengths are considered in tandem with institutional vision and mission, the surrounding community, and work–life integration. First-generation aspiring senior leaders may feel intimidated by authority, react passively, and stay in the background without thorough self-reflection and feedback on these factors.

Quinn and Spreitzer (2006) defined the *fundamental state of leadership* to describe factors that tip the balance toward excellence. He called on leaders to "honestly answer four transformative questions: Am I results centered? Am I other focused? Am I internally directed? Am I externally open?" (Quinn & Spreitzer, 2006, p. 105). These questions can light the path toward senior leadership in higher education.

Each institution's mission and vision includes themes of teaching and learning. Some may also include research and scholarship, social justice and equity, and advancement of or service to particular communities. The mission and vision are, indeed, the core drivers for all traditions and innovations, processes and procedures, and measures of success at the institution. They define the culture of an organization and dictate how decisions will be made. Although nuanced approaches exist within units, it is the responsibility of senior leaders to carry out the mission and vision of their institution. Advancing the mission and vision of the institution is the key to being "results centered." Senior leaders should spend time aligning talent and resources toward these results. Great leaders know it is fundamental to put the collective good first. The needs and goals of the institution must come before personal benefits and desires. "When we put the collective good first, others reward us with their trust and respect" (Quinn & Spreitzer, 2006, p. 109).

The success of an institution is certainly tied closely to the success of the surrounding community. It is incumbent upon senior leaders to be trustworthy liaisons to local public officials, thoughtful neighbors to local residents, and productive partners with local business owners. Effective leaders in higher education should also seek personal fulfillment within the community in which they live and work. School systems that match family needs, available hobbies and activities with which to engage, volunteer opportunities, and even shopping areas that meet needs are all factors that contribute to this alignment. Leaders who are seen at the local grocer, salon, or sporting event are likely taking the time to develop relationships that will make a difference in the workplace as well. Each connection may lead to an insight or relationship that can help advance a priority for the institution and community.

Quinn and Spreitzer (2006) wrote, "To become more internally directed is to clarify our core values and increase our integrity, confidence, and authenticity" (p. 109). Over the course of a career, senior leaders should continually reflect on successes and failures to evaluate their leadership values alignment with the institution and the community. Mentorship encourages a more profound examination of values and action alignment through ongoing feedback and deliberation. Further, mentors may be present in both the higher education enterprise and within the community.

Hewlett (2014) conducted a national, cross-industry study that concluded that, when it comes to successful leadership, executive presence is the one thing more important than merit. The core factor of executive presence is *gravitas*, defined "as the ability to exude integrity, calmness, and confidence under the most pressing circumstances" (Hewlett, 2014, p. 268). Staying true to one's own values as a leader will affirm their executive presence, allowing one to speak with purpose, not impulse.

Gravitas also requires that highly effective senior leaders practice listening for cues and signals that may challenge them to hear uncomfortable truths or pivot from the original plan. It is important to understand when a decision has negatively impacted a constituent. Undoubtedly this leads to great innovation in the workplace, but also builds trust among teams and communities. For example, noticing a shift in energy during a team retreat may be an opportunity to read the room, change tactics, and check in with team members about the impact of a decision and the interest in moving forward. What the leader may read as the team becoming tired and disengaged may actually be evidence of the team members deeply considering new challenges and digging for the creativity to design solutions.

Engaging that same depth of listening in all aspects of life also helps one achieve work–life integration. Every leader has personal obligations. It can be beneficial to share with colleagues some elements of personal interests and obligations without going into excruciating detail. For example, one might verbalize the priority of attending a child's sporting event without discussing the negative behavior the child demonstrates when the parent/leader is not present. These priorities may mean that the leader misses a campus program but commits to attendance the following night. An appropriate level of transparency can help a leader gain trust and understanding from their team members. Successful work–life integration is fluid, ever-changing based on the evolving nature of one's life and demands of the organization. Highly effective senior leaders pay attention to external stimuli that may signal a need for change.

Authentically aligned senior leaders choose work within environments and communities that nurture their interests and allow their values to be put into action. They are able to command accountability for mission-driven results while practicing compassion. They engage in the communities of which they are a member as a matter of personal fulfillment, as well as strategic relationship building. Authentically aligned leaders inspire others to high performance.

Conclusion

The academy will continue to call on innovative, compassionate problem solvers to meet the complex and evolving challenges of higher education. First-generation aspiring senior leaders can prepare to fill this demand by designing intentional pathways for gaining critical experience, technical competence, self-awareness, and industry expertise. Taking the time to reflect on how one successfully met mid-level goals will allow aspiring senior leaders to develop such plans for traveling the path to senior leadership. Embracing lifelong learning, seeking growth opportunities, and continually expanding one's skill set and competencies are all salient in creating a navigable path.

While developing plans for a path to travel, first-generation professionals should find ways to authentically incorporate the various identities, interests, experiences, and interests within their world. This may feel daunting, as one looks around seeking others like them. However, it is doable and necessary to pave the way for future leaders ahead. Those aspiring to become senior leaders should keep in mind that adaptability, creativity, persistence, and confidence are essential to successfully navigating the nuances of the higher education landscape.

Finding one's fit, one's community, and one's ability to integrate work and life is essential. Finding the path that most aligns with one's passions, strengths, and goals is salient to success. There are multiple pathways to travel toward senior leadership. These is no one way to create a pathway to senior leadership; rather, aspiring senior leaders must find the path that most authentically and genuinely speaks to them.

Questions for Reflection

1. What do you know about your leadership style? What are your leadership strengths and growth opportunities?
2. What steps do you need to take to create a plan to address growth opportunities and enhance existing capacities?
3. What theory informs your daily work? How does your practice build on that theory?
4. If needed, how might you pursue an advanced degree?
5. How can you engage professionally and contribute academically?
6. Which of your personal identities feels most salient in your work environment?
7. How do you "lift as you climb?"
8. What are your personal interests and priorities for work–life integration?

References

Abdulahad, S., Booker, A. A., Hairston, S. L., James, T. D., King, C., Lander, T., Paige, T. R., Reed, C., Sturdivant, J., Ward, L., & Young-Waters, A. (2018). *The table: Stories from Black women in student affairs*. The Table Books.

American Council on Education. (2017). *American college president study*. http://www.aceacps.org

Bolman, L. G., & Gallos, J. V. (2011). *Reframing academic leadership*. Jossey-Bass.

Bowman, N. (2010). Cultivating future fundraisers of color at historically Black colleges and universities. *International Journal of Education Advancement, 10*(3), 230–234. https://doi.org/10.1057/ijea.2010.19

Brown, S. (2019, February 14). Nearly half of undergraduates are students of color. But Black students lag behind. *The Chronicle of Higher Education*. https://www.chronicle.com/article/Nearly-Half-of-Undergraduates/245692

Carbado, D., Crenshaw, K., Mays, V., & Tomlinson, B. (2013). Intersectionality: Mapping the movements of a theory. *Du Bois Review: Social Science Research on Race, 10*(2), 303–312. https://doi.org/10.1017/S1742058X13000349

Crimmin, N., & Dobrowski, P. (2016). Leadership and strategic planning: A blend of visionary and practical. In A. Hecht & J. B. Pina (Eds.), *AVP: Leading from the unique role of associate/assistant vice president for student affairs* (pp. 57–77). NASPA–Student Affairs Administrators in Higher Education.

Deloitte Center for Higher Education Excellence. (2017). *Pathways to the university presidency: The future of higher education leadership*. Deloitte University Press.

Deming, D. J., & Figlio, D. (2016). Accountability in U.S. education: Applying lessons from K–12 experience to higher education. *Journal of Economic Perspectives, 30*(3), 33–55. https://doi.org/10.1257/jep.30.3.33

Dukes, C. M. (2011). Leading with vision and practicality. In G. W. Dungy & S. E. Ellis (Eds.), *Exceptional senior student affairs administrators' leadership: Strategies and competencies for success* (pp. 210–217). NASPA–Student Affairs Administrators in Higher Education.

Dungy, G. W., & Ellis, S. E. (2011). *Exceptional senior student affairs administrators' leadership: Strategies and competencies for success*. NASPA–Student Affairs Administrators in Higher Education.

Eddy, P. L., & Garza Mitchell, R. L. (2017). Preparing community college leaders to meet tomorrow's challenges. *Journal for the Study of Postsecondary and Tertiary Education, 2*, 127–145. https://doi.org/10.28945/3884

Eismann, L. (2016). *First-generation students and job success*. National Association of Colleges and Employers. https://www.naceweb.org/job-market/special-populations/first-generation-students-and-job-success

Freeman, S., Jr., & Kochan, F. K. (2012). Academic pathways to university leadership: Presidents' descriptions of their doctoral education. *International Journal of Doctoral Studies, 7*, 93–124. https://doi.org/10.28945/1567

Gasman, M., Abiola, U., & Travers, C. (2015). Diversity and senior leadership at elite institutions of higher education. *Journal of Diversity in Higher Education, 8*(1), 1–14. https://doi.org/10.1037/a0038872

Hamrick, F. A., Evans, N. J., & Schuh, J. H. (2002). *Foundations of student affairs practice: How philosophy, theory, and research strengthen educational outcomes*. Jossey-Bass.

Heifetz, R. A., & Linsky, M. (2002). *Leadership on the line*. Harvard Business School Press.

Hewlett, S. A. (2014). *Executive presence: The missing link between merit and success*. Harper Collins Publishers.

Hill, L. H., & Wheat, C. A. (2017). The influence of mentorship and role models on university women leaders' career paths to university presidency. *The Qualitative Report, 22*(8), 2090–2111. https://nsuworks.nova.edu/tqr/vol22/iss8/2

Johnson, H. J. (2017). *Pipelines, pathways, and institutional leadership: An update on the status of women in higher education.* American Council on Education.

Joshi, A., & Mangette, H. (2018). Unmasking of impostor syndrome. *Journal of Research, Assessment, and Practice in Higher Education, 3*(1), 1–8. https://ecommons.udayton.edu/jraphe/vol3/iss1/3

Kezar, A. J., & Holcombe, E. M. (2017). *Shared leadership in higher education: Important lessons from research and practice.* American Council on Education.

Kimbrough, W. M. (2011). Just the facts. In G. W. Dungy & S. E. Ellis (Eds.), *Exceptional senior student affairs administrators' leadership: Strategies and competencies for success* (pp. 183–187). NASPA–Student Affairs Administrators in Higher Education.

Lawson, C. J. (2007). Crisis communication. In E. L. Zdziarski, N. W. Dunkel, & J. M. Rollo (Eds.), *Campus crisis management: A comprehensive guide to planning, prevention, response, and recovery* (pp. 97–120). Jossey-Bass.

Matthew, P. A. (2016, November 23). What is faculty diversity worth to a university? *The Atlantic.* https://www.theatlantic.com/education/archive/2016/11/what-is-faculty-diversity-worth-to-a-university/508334

McChesney, J. (2018, May). *Representation and pay of women of color in the higher education workforce.* College and University Professional Association for Human Resources. https://www.cupahr.org/wp-content/uploads/CUPA-HR-Brief-Women-Of-Color-1.pdf

Middleton, C. R. (2016, June 7). LGBTQ talent and institutional success. *LGBTQ Presidents in Higher Education.* http://www.lgbtqpresidents.org/blog

National Conference of State Legislatures. (2019). *Higher education legislation in 2019.* http://www.ncsl.org/research/education/higher-education-legislation-in-2019.aspx

Olsen, Z. (2017, August 30). Don't let a crisis become your legacy. Inside Higher Education. https://www.insidehighered.com/blogs/call-action-marketing-and-communications-higher-education/dont-let-crisis-become-your-legacy

Parkman, A. (2016). The imposter phenomenon in higher education: Incidence and impact. *Journal of Higher Education, 16*(1), 51–60.

Quinn, R. E., & Spreitzer, G. M. (2006). Entering the fundamental state of leadership: A framework for the positive transformation of self and others. In R. J. Burke & C. Cooper (Eds.), *Inspiring Leaders* (pp. 83–99). Routledge. https://doi.org/10.4324/9780203013199

Ruben, B. D., De Lisi, R., & Gigliotti, R. A. (2017). *A guide for leaders in higher education: Core concepts, competencies, and tools.* Stylus.

Schipani, C. A., Sworkin, T. M., Kwolek-Folland, A., & Maurer, V. G. (2009). Pathways for women to obtain positions of organizational leadership: The significance of mentoring and networking. *Duke Journal of Gender Law and Policy, 16*(1), 89–136. https://scholarship.law.duke.edu/djglp/vol16/iss1/3

Selingo, J. (2015). *The view from the top: What presidents think about financial sustainability, student outcomes, and the future of higher education.* The Chronicle of Higher Education.

Senge, P. M. (1990). *The fifth discipline: The art and practice of the learning organization.* Doubleday/Currency.

Trammell, J. B. (2014, May/June). LGBT challenges in higher education today: 5 core principles for success. *Trusteeship.* https://agb.org/trusteeship-article/lgbt-challenges-in-higher-education-today-5-core-principles-for-success

Zaccaro, S. J., & Banks, D. (2004). Leader visioning and adaptability: Bridging the gap between research and practice on developing the ability to manage change. *Human Resource Management, 43*(4), 367–380. https://doi.org/10.1002/hrm.20030

THE AUTHORS

Mary Blanchard Wallace, PhD, serves as the assistant vice president for student experience at the University of Alabama at Birmingham. With more than 27 years of work in higher education, she has served at the University of Arkansas at Monticello, the University of Tulsa, Texas Woman's University, and Louisiana State University. The first in her family to attend college, Blanchard Wallace earned a BS in liberal arts, with a concentration in psychology and biology, and an MA in student personnel services from Northwestern State University in Natchitoches, Louisiana. She received her PhD in human resource education and workforce development from Louisiana State University. Currently, Blanchard Wallace serves as the cochair of the Research and Scholarship Committee of NASPA's Student Affairs Partnering with Academic Affairs Knowledge Community.

Sonja Ardoin, PhD, is a learner, educator, facilitator, and author. Proud of her hometown of Vidrine, Louisiana, her working-class background, her Cajun roots, and her journey from first-generation college student to PhD recipient, Ardoin holds degrees from Louisiana State University, Florida State, and North Carolina State. She considers herself a scholar–practitioner of higher education; she served as an administrator for 10 years before shifting to faculty in 2015 and is currently associate professor and program director in the student affairs administration program at Appalachian State

University. Ardoin studies social class identity, college access and success for rural and first-generation college students, student and women's leadership, and career preparation and pathways in higher education and student affairs.

Willie Banks, PhD, serves as the vice chancellor for student affairs at the University of California, Irvine. He has held several administrative positions at Indiana State University, Cleveland State University, and the University of Georgia. Banks received his bachelor's degree from Mercer University and his master's and PhD degrees in college student affairs administration from the University of Georgia.

Danette D. Buie, EdD, is a diversity business partner at Coursera, an EdTech company in the Bay Area committed to providing universal access to world-class learning. She has more than 10 years of experience in education that ranges from K–12 to community-based organizations, public policy, and higher education. Buie is the first in her family to graduate from college and pursue a graduate degree. Her doctoral research focused on the persistence of underrepresented (first-generation, minoritized, and low-income) students in college and their participation in community-based organizations. Through her research, Buie identifies as a social constructionist and enjoys studying the social construction of knowledge and its impact on reality and marginalized people who are not members of dominant culture.

Ainsley Carry, PhD, is the vice president for students at the University of British Columbia (UBC) in Vancouver, Canada. He has more than 25 years of experience in college administration, serving as vice president for student affairs at Auburn University and the University of Southern California before his role at UBC.

Doris Ching, PhD, served as vice president for student affairs and associate dean of education at the University of Hawai`i (UH) and interim chancellor of UH-West Oʻahu, where she strongly advocated for student success and equal rights for all students. She was the first woman of color and first Asian American and Pacific Islander to be elected president of NASPA–Student Affairs Administrators in Higher Education. The first in her family to complete a college degree, Ching received her EdD from Arizona State University and her BEd and MEd from UH-Mānoa.

Claudia García-Louis, PhD, is an assistant professor in the Education Leadership and Policy Studies Department at the University of Texas San Antonio. Her interdisciplinary research approach seeks to disrupt negative stereotypes about Latinx students, minoritized populations, and underrepresented students through the critical incorporation of a culturally appropriate, asset-based methodology. Her goals are to expand the definitions of *Latinidad* and *Blackness* in higher education, to make a critical contribution to a newly formed line of inquiry that explores the educational experiences of AfroLatinx individuals, and to conduct research that highlights Latinx intragroup heterogeneity and the experiences of Latina-mamí-scholars.

Brian O. Hemphill, PhD, proudly serves as Old Dominion University's ninth president. Since joining this university community on July 1, 2021, he has been an unwavering champion for innovation and a true advocate of student success. His vision is to propel Old Dominion into national and international prominence with a keen focus on transformational research and world-class teaching. A tenant of Hemphill's leadership is for Old Dominion University to become an entrepreneurial and forward-focused public research university.

John R. Jones III, PhD, is the vice president for student affairs at the University of Alabama at Birmingham (UAB). Before joining UAB, he served as vice chancellor for student affairs at the University of North Carolina Pembroke. He also was associate vice president in the Division of Student Affairs and Enrollment Management at Northern Illinois University and assistant vice chancellor and associate dean of students in the Division of Student Life and Diversity at Indiana University Purdue University Indianapolis. Jones, whose roots are in Chapel Hill, North Carolina, received a BS degree in applied mathematics from Appalachian State University. He attended The University of Iowa, where he obtained a master's and a PhD in higher education administration.

Brandi Hephner LaBanc, EdD, is the vice chancellor for student affairs and campus life at the University of Massachusetts Amherst. With over 25 years of experience in higher education, she has served as vice chancellor for student affairs and professor of higher education at The University of Mississippi, and held multiple administrative roles at Northern Illinois University, Arizona State University, the University of North Carolina Wilmington, Baldwin-Wallace College, and The University of Akron. As a first-generation student she pursued an accounting degree from The University of Akron prior to graduate study in higher education administration at Kent State University, then as a first-generation professional she earned her EdD from Northern Illinois University. She is a NASPA Pillar of the Profession and has been recognized by her graduate institutions for her leadership in higher education.

Darris R. Means, PhD, is an associate professor of higher education at the University of Pittsburgh. His scholarship focuses on postsecondary education access and success for Black students. Means's research appears in *The Review of Higher Education, Journal of College Student Development, Teachers College Record, Journal of Student Affairs Research and Practice*, and *Journal of Diversity in Higher Education*.

D'Andra Mull, PhD, is vice president for student life at the University of Florida. In this role she is responsible for creating pathways for student success and building comprehensively excellent student experiences that allow students to engage, transform, and thrive. With more than 20 years of experience in higher education, Mull served at Kent State University, Michigan State University, and The Ohio State University. She is a first-generation college graduate with a Bachelor of Arts in political science and criminal justice studies from Kent State University, a Master of Arts in higher, adult, and lifelong education from Michigan State University, and a PhD in educational policy and leadership from The Ohio State University.

Samantha Payton serves as the director of research, assessment, and planning for student affairs at The University of Mississippi. She has more than 10 years of experience in assessment and evaluation, using her background in biological sciences, forensic sciences, and student affairs to approach complex questions in higher education from a multidisciplinary, rigorously scientific, and outcomes-driven perspective. Payton's previous research and publications address biological resources conservation, residential curriculum, employee climate, and student union facilities management.

La'Tonya Rease Miles, PhD, is the dean of student affairs at Menlo College in the San Francisco Bay Area. She is a proud first-generation graduate of the University of Maryland, College Park; she received her PhD in English from the University of California, Los Angeles. Her research interests include first-generation college narratives and the representation of first-generation students in popular culture.

Patricia S. Smith serves as associate vice president for student life at Radford University. She believes in the transformative potential of higher education and dedicates her time and efforts toward social justice in the academy and in her community. Smith currently works with engagement, wellness, and inclusion efforts, paying keen attention to creating meaningful relationships that yield student success.

Robin M. Williamson, PhD, is the vice president for student affairs at the University of Central Arkansas. She is passionate about first-year experience, community engagement, and first-generation student access and success.

INDEX

Figures and tables are indicated by f and t following the page number.